Invisible Queen©

Biography of Sophia Charlotte
Queen of Britain and Ireland
1761-1818

By

Stephanie E. Myers

R.J. Myers Publishing Company
www.myerspublishing.com

Published by R.J. Myers Publishing & Consulting Company

ISBN #: 978-1-884108-05-1

Layout and Design: Initial Design & Media, LLC
Copy Editor: Fern Robinson

Cover Portrait by
Esther Denner, German painter ca. 1710-1779
Art in the Invisible Queen, is in the public domain

*"Prudence imposes silence,
and that little dear word Silence
has so often been my friend in necessity,
that I make it my constant companion."*

Queen Sophia Charlotte

Dedication

This book is dedicated to my husband Roy J. Myers, my mother Estella E. Lee, our children, grandchildren and their spouses.

Treasure your heritage. It strengthens us all.

Acknowledgements

Many thanks to my love and publisher Roy J. Myers for your support, creativity and editorial review. To Richard Warr, Initial Design & Media, thank you for your creative design, patience and layout for various projects, over the years. Thanks to Copy Editor Fern Robinson for your editing services. And, a special thanks to our readers Joy Price Ferro, Paula G. Leftwich, Anne Morrison, Audrey Hinton Richardson, Lynley Cejas and Ashley Casserly. We appreciate your support, insights and feedback.

Table of Contents

Introduction

One evening, my husband and I decided to research our genealogical backgrounds on the web. We surfed to web sites that connected our lineage to Ghana, Cameroon, Ethiopia, Germany, England, and various regions in North America. While we were researching, we came across a picture of a woman identified as Queen Sophia Charlotte of Mecklenburg-Strelitz, Germany. Her 18th -century portrait by artist Thomas Frye, appeared to us to be a mixed-race woman, with facial features that resembled many of our friends and family members.

We were surprised to learn the woman we were looking at was a German princess known as Sophia Charlotte (herein referred to as Charlotte) who at the age of 17, married King George III of Britain. This woman reigned as Queen of England and Ireland, for 57 years but, we had never heard of her. She was Queen during the late 1700's and early 1800's, when America was only a group of colonies. This was a period of history when England and other parts of Europe, were involved in the Atlantic slave trade, and kidnapped African people and sent them to the New World for a lifetime of enslavement.

Further research into the history of King George III and Queen Charlotte, revealed that they ruled England for more than five decades. We realized that historians, politicians and the media had forgotten to mention that Queen Charlotte was a colleague of leading Abolitionists and that she personally advocated for an end to the slave trade. In addition, history teachers didn't teach us that Charlotte's husband King George III issued the first Emancipation Proclamation to free enslaved people in the American colonies, in 1774, about 90 years before President Abraham Lincoln issued a similar Emancipation Proclamation, after the Civil War. This book tries to fill in the gaps of history left out by many history classes in the United States and Europe.

Queen Charlotte as the wife of King George III and Queen of England, reigned with grace and dignity and there were no scandals associated with her tenure and behavior. She was a diplomat, proud mother and caregiver for her husband who suffered from a serious illness that affected his behavior. She was also a botanist, a musician and a woman of faith.

The African American Registry, a non-profit organization, describes Charlotte as, "England's First Black Queen." The website continues, "Queen Charlotte made many contributions to Britain as it is today, though the evidence is not obvious or well publicized. Her African bloodline in the British Royal family is not common knowledge." Other sources unapologetically describe Charlotte as a black woman including: (1) Charlotte Sophia: Myth, Madness and the Moor, by Tina Andrews; (2) Mulatto Queen, by Kimba Hudson; and (3) Black Royals, Queen Charlotte, a research paper by Joysetta Marsh Pearse and

Fatimah White. There is also a powerful television documentary about Queen Charlotte, produced by the Public Broadcasting System, based on research by Mario de Valdes Cocom, titled <u>Blurred Racial Lines of Famous Families.</u>

To be fair, there are those who dispute Charlotte's Moorish or African heritage and researchers who claim there is no evidence that proves she was mixed race. Cynics say if she did have Black heritage it would have been so small it wasn't traceable. However, for this book we are relying on historic reports, visual images, and art history that reveal a pattern that leads to the conclusion that Queen Charlotte was a woman with Moorish/African heritage.

Queen Charlotte is a historic figure who might have been downplayed because she was an educated, talented woman who lived during a time when most women were not allowed to get an education, and were barred from politics. Whatever the reason, one thing is clear, regardless of her ethnicity Charlotte was a knowledgeable woman who employed her skills in many different areas and left an important legacy. Some of her outstanding accomplishments are:

- Wife to the King of England for 57 years
- Mother of 15 children
- Spoke four languages
- Played instruments and sang with musical groups
- Was an early patron of Mozart
- Has cities and other areas named for her in America, and other parts of the world
- Supported the Abolitionist movement to end slavery
- Entertained world leaders at Court, including U.S. Presidents and diplomats
- Was a skilled botanist and expanded the Kew botanical gardens
- Supported a school to teach girls embroidery
- Helped establish the first public maternity hospital for poor women
- Had a comet named for her
- Established a home for widows and fatherless girls
- Served as caregiver for her husband King George II, who suffered from a long-term illness

As a princess raised in Germany, Charlotte had privileges and advantages. She learned early to have compassion for others and stood by her husband King George III when he was heavily criticized for the British losing the American Revolutionary War. She also stood behind a team of Abolitionists who fought slavery for decades. Even though she was Queen, Charlotte was bullied by mean critiques from members of the British Court and the press who called her ugly because of her Negroid features. But, she survived it all and most importantly, she lent her voice to the side of human rights, compassion and fairness.

This author believes Queen Charlotte can inspire individuals of diverse backgrounds to do pursue great accomplishments, regardless of race, gender, religion, status in life and national origin. As you read this book, you can reach your own conclusion about why Charlotte is, "The Invisible Queen" and you can decide if she deserves recognition. It is my belief Sophia Charlotte of Mecklenburg-Strelitz was one of the most important women of the 18th Century and deserves to be taken seriously by all. Therefore, it is my honor to present Queen Sophia Charlotte (1744-1818), Queen of the United Kingdom of Britain and Ireland, from 1761-1818.

Dr. Stephanie E. Myers
Washington, D.C.

Queen Sophia Charlotte

**Portrait by
Thomas Frye, 1710-1762**

CHAPTER ONE
Charlotte's Early Years

Imagine living in a castle your entire life and being raised as a German princess, as part of a Royal Family. This was the life of Princess Sophia Charlotte, a lovely, energetic girl with a light-brown complexion, large brown eyes, thick curly hair and pretty, full lips. Charlotte was born May 19, 1744, in the picturesque City of Mirow, in Mecklenburg-Strelitz, northeast Germany, 150 miles west of the famous City of Berlin. Her family was known as the House of Mecklenburg Strelitz and her community was called the Grand Duchy of Mecklenburg-Strelitz. The historic city of Mirow was dotted with old castles, churches, villages, market towns and German cultural centers of learning. Her family were political leaders of the region, with a heritage that went back hundreds of years.

Location of Mecklenburg-Strelitz, North-East Germany[1]

Charlotte was eighth in a family of ten children, born to the dynamic Duke Charles Louis Frederick, (February 1708–June 5, 1752) and his capable wife Duchess Elizabeth Albertina (August 4, 1713–June 29, 1761). Prior to her birth, her parents had lost three baby girls who died at childbirth so, when Charlotte was born healthy, the family was understandably thrilled and she received a great deal of love and attention. Charlotte's parents spent a lot of time preparing Charlotte and her siblings to be solid members of the German ruling class. Her brothers and sisters were: Duchess Christiana, Duchess Karoline, Duke Adolf Friedrich IV, Duchess Elizabeth Christine, Duchess Sophie Louise, Duke Charles II, Duke Ernst Gottlob, Duke Gotthelf, and Duke George Augustus. Her oldest brother, Duke Adolf Friedrich was heir to the Mecklenburg-Stelitz empire, behind their father Duke Charles Louis Frederick and he took over the leadership of the family when their parents passed away.

Charlotte's Education

As a young girl, Charlotte loved school. She was tutored in German, French and Italian languages by Dr. Genzmer, a Lutheran scholar who was knowledgeable about natural history, philosophy, and literature.[2] Charlotte learned how to fluently speak and translate the three languages she studied—a skill that came in handy later. She was particularly fond of history, botany, and music. According to biographer W.C. Oulton, one of Charlotte's delights was needlework and being involved in household affairs. [3] In fact, needlework was very popular in her household and everyone did it, including her grandfather.

Charlotte's Grandfather Duke Adolphus Frederick III[4]

One humorous story handed down within Charlotte's family was about her grandfather Duke Adolphus Frederick III (1686-1752) and his love of needlework. In 1736, a young military leader who came to be known as Frederick the Great, Crown Prince of Prussia, paid a visit to Charlotte's family. When he arrived, Frederick was openly surprised to find Duke Adolphus—Charlotte's Grandfather--embroidering a beautiful dressing gown. Frederick later joked about the incident since just as in modern times, it was unusual for men to embroider gowns. [5]   But, Duke Adolphus enjoyed his embroidery and his interest in

Charlotte's Early Years

designing clothes helped Charlotte to develop an interest in needlework and embroidery. Charlotte used her design and sewing skills, throughout her life.

When Charlotte was 15, her parents enrolled her in a prestigious private school called 'Herford Ministry of Westphalia.' In the 1700's, it was unusual for girls to attend school. The boys went to school but, most young ladies in Germany received no education at all. Herford Ministry was a Christian convent established in the 16th century, where nuns and priests served as teachers for female students from upper-class families. Charlotte and her classmates were taught religion, classical European history and were exposed to a wide range of scholars and philosophers. While Charlotte did not plan to be a nun, she was received religious and non-religious training and she impressed her teachers with her studiousness. [6] On March 7, 1760, Charlotte was given the high honor of being invested as a Canoness of the Ministry. Miriam Webster dictionary notes a, "Canoness is a woman living in a community under a religious rule but, not under a perpetual vow."[7] This honor was reserved for women and girls who were not nuns but, were committed to living simple and religious lives.

Years later in 1786, when Charlotte was Queen of England, she told Fanny Burney, one of her ladies-in-waiting, a story about the convents and monasteries at Herford Ministry. She recalled, "We had Protestant nunneries in Germany. I belonged to one which was under the Imperial protection."[8] Note: Fanny Burney was known as, "Keeper of the Robes" for Queen Charlotte from 1786-1791. Frances kept extensive diaries and is regarded as one of the most famous well-known female writers of her era.[9]

Charlotte's School, the Herford Ministry of Westphalia, Germany[10]

Charlotte's education at Herford Ministry prepared her to be a critical thinker. In 1760, while at school she wrote a letter partly in German and partly in French, to a pen-pal she addressed as "Right Reverend Fellow Countryman." She wrote that she was "sending back the first two volumes" of books he had shared with her and requested more. Charlotte wrote, "I also return the first part of the works of Voltaire, but, he is for me not a quality man, and I do not want anything more of his."[11] Charlotte's comments were bold since Voltaire was one of France's greatest Enlightenment writers, with a tremendous influence on politicians and philosophers. While Voltaire was often controversial with faith institutions, he was a leading intellectual of his times.[12] The fact Charlotte was reading books by Voltaire and had opinions about his writings, provides insight into the quality of her education, her natural intellect and ability to analyze what she read. She was a smart, well-read girl.

Musical Training

Charlotte's father Duke Charles Frederick taught her how to play various instruments and to sing and harmonize in a choral group. She played the harpsichord, a keyboard instrument similar to a piano, and she played the glockenspiel, an instrument with two small hammers that tapped out melodic music.[13] During family gatherings at Mirow Castle, Charlotte accompanied her father, brothers, and sisters when they sang together in a family ensemble. Her natural talent for music became important later, during her reign as Queen of England.

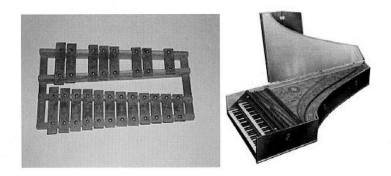

Charlotte Played the Glockenspiel and Harpsichord

CHAPTER ONE
Charlotte's Early Years

Charlotte's Letter to King of Prussia

Frederick the Great of Prussia, Portrait by Anton Graff, 1781[14]

As a Canoness at the Herford Ministry, Charlotte learned compassion for people, animals and nature. She also developed a strong sense of social responsibility, for people in need. Charlotte demonstrated her compassion when she was 14, and there was a major conflict in Europe known as the Seven Years War.[15] This war, that began in 1754, is the first recorded global conflict and involved Prussia, Austria, Britain, France and Spain. Frederick the Great, her Grandfather's friend, was the leader of Prussia and the top military leader in the war. In 1757, Charlotte learned that Frederick the Great's military strategy had led to fighting in the cities of Saxony and Hanover—areas close to where she lived. To her horror, some of her neighbors in Mecklenburg-Strelitz were being harmed by the war's battles. Although she was only 14, Charlotte wrote a strong letter of protest to His Majesty Frederick the Great, and expressed her concerns about the toll the war was having on her neighbor. (See attached letter)

Charlotte's letter to Frederick the Great provides insight into her awareness of the limited role women and girls had in politics, and showed she was aware of the unusual nature of her protest. In her letter, Charlotte commented that Frederick the Great might find her letter to be "unbecoming of her sex," but, she sent the letter anyway. This willingness to speak out against the war showed self-confidence and strength of conviction. While it is not known if Frederick the Great ever responded to her concerns directly, her letter was circulated throughout Europe and caused quite a stir. Subsequent actions on the part of Frederick the Great indicate he did order his troops to refrain from violence in some of the areas near Mecklenburg-Strelitz. Perhaps Charlotte's letter did have an influence on her Grandfather's friend but, whether it did not the fact Charlotte wrote the letter showed that a 14-year old teenage girl could have a voice.

CHAPTER ONE
Charlotte's Early Years

Letter from Charlotte to Frederick the Great About Seven Years War[16]

May it please your Majesty,

"I am at a loss whether I should congratulate or condole with you on your late victory; since the same success which has covered you with laurels, has overspread the country of Mecklenburgh with desolation. I know, Sire, that it seems unbecoming my sex, in this age of vicious refinement, to feel for one's country, to lament the horrors of war, or wish for the return of peace. I know you may think it more properly my province to study the arts of pleasing; or to inspect subjects of a more domestic nature: but, however, unbecoming it may be in me, I cannot resist the desire of interceding for this unhappy people. It was but a very few years ago, that this territory wore the most pleasing appearance. The country was cultivated, the peasants looked cheerful, and the towns abounded with riches and festivity! 'What an alteration, at present, from such a charming scene! I am not expert at description-nor can my fimcy add horrors to the pirture; but sure even conquerors themselves would weep at the hideous prospects now before me.

The whole country, my dear country, now lies one frightful waste, presenting only objects to excite terror, pity, and despair! The business of the husbandman and the shepherd are quite discontinued; the husbandman and the shepherd are become soldiers themselves, and help- to ravage the soil they formerly cultivated. The towns are inhabited only by old men, women, and children; perhaps here and there a warrior, by wounds or loss 'lf limbs, rendered unfit for service, left at his door; _his little children hang round him, ask an history of every wound, and grow themselves soldiers before they find strength tor the field. But this were nothing, did we not feel the alternate insolence of either army? it happens to advance or retreat in pursuing the operations of the campaign: ---It is impossible to express the confusion, even those who call themselves our friends, create. Even those from whom we expect redress, oppress us with new calamities.

From your justice, therefore it is, that we hope relief; to you, even children and women may complain, whose humanity stoops to the meanest petition, and whose power is capable of repressing the patent injustice.

"Iam, Sire," &c.

CHAPTER ONE
Charlotte's Early Years

Living in a Castle

Charlotte's family home was Mirow Castle, a place known by the Germans as "Schloss Mirow" or "Location of Peace." Mir is a Slavic word, which stands for "joy or peace."[17] The castle was in the town of Mirow, near the City of Mecklenburg-Strelitz, 150 miles west of the City of Berlin. The area was a large, somewhat desolate area prized for beauty and simplicity bordered on the east by Poland; on the north by the Baltic Sea; on the west by Lower Saxony; and on the south by the City of Brandenberg. The city still exists and travelers can visit it in Germany today.

Mirow Castle, Mecklenburg-Strelitz, Germany[18]

Mirow Castle was built in 1707 by architect Joachim Borchman, who was commissioned by Charlotte's grandfather Duke Adolphus, to build a unique building. The castle sits in the middle of an English-style park and became known for its beautifully decorated ballroom and Red Salon, lined with silk Chinese-style wall coverings. After the German Revolution in the early 1900's when the Mecklenburg Royal Families were removed from power, Mirow Castle became a museum and was later used as a Russian granary. During the 20th Century from 1951-1978, the castle was used as a retirement home however, in the late 1970's, a Russian named Duke Georg Alexander, worked to restore its earlier beauty. [19] Beginning in 1999, renovation began on the castle that was scheduled for completion in 2014.[20] Charlotte's family also owned a second palace known as the Palace at Neustrelitz, located near the region of Mecklenburg-Strelitz. Charlotte and her family lived in both places during different times of the year.

CHAPTER ONE
Charlotte's Early Years

Nature Rich Environment

The Mecklenburg Lake area where Charlotte and her brothers and sisters grew up, was nature-rich, with beautiful parks and clear-water lakes, filled with fish. They could walk to tree-filled woods and local gardens, where they learned how to grow plants, and work with animals. The Mecklenburg Lake area has 1,000 miles of coastline where the lakes, rivers, and canals flow into hundreds of beaches and bluffs. Many varieties of birds migrate annually to the lakes, including eagles, black storks, herons, and thousands of cranes and wild geese. Today, the area is known as National Muritz Park, and tourists from all over the world travel to the park to enjoy boating, kayaking, camping and the beautiful natural landscape.[21]

Birds in Mecklenburg Lakes Area
Double Breasted Comorant Black Stork, in Mecklenburg[22]

Charlotte and her brothers and sisters played in the waters of Müritz Lake, known as the "small sea" linked into waterways between Berlin and Hamburg. They could boat across Muritz Lake to see the impressive sea and landscapes, that connected directly into the heart of Mecklenburg-Strelitz. Today, visitors can see some of the birds Charlotte saw as a child, including storks, common herons, cranes, ospreys and sea eagles, as well as red deer, otters, beavers and raccoons. Visitors can also see the historic buildings in Mirow, that were there during Charlotte's era, including old churches, manors and castles in surrounding small villages and towns.

CHAPTER ONE
Charlotte's Early Years

Modern Photo of Mecklenburg Lake District[23]

CHAPTER TWO
Family Background

Mecklenburg Family

As head of the House of Mecklenburg, Charlotte's father, Duke Charles Frederick ruled historic northeast Germany, during the early 1700's. Some of the cities under his authority were the Cities of Dresden and Berlin. The City of Dresden is situated in a valley on the River Elbe, near the border of the Czech Republic, and the City of Berlin is the capital and largest city of Germany. Berlin is the second largest city in the European Union, with over 3 million residents.

Close-Up Portrait of Charlotte, by artist Alan Ramsey

The Mecklenburg family was one of the most powerful families in Germany. As a result, females in the family were considered by European rulers to be desirable wives. This led to several Mecklenburg girls marrying significant leaders. During this time in history, arranged marriages were very common and young women were sent to marry men who had power and money. For example, Charlotte's niece Luise married King Friedrich Wilhelm III of Prussia in 1793; and a second niece Friedrike married King Ernst August of Hanover in 1815. The arranged marriages of girls in the family to powerful men who lived in different parts of Europe, enabled men in the Mecklenburg family to pursue military careers in the armies of their brother-in-law's, and to receive rapid career advancement. This led to personal wealth and high-profile government posts for the men.[24]

CHAPTER TWO
Family Background

Charlotte's Father

Charlotte's father, Duke Charles Louis Frederick (1708–1752) was born in Mecklenburg-Strelitz, as the only son of Duke Adolphus Frederick and his third wife Princess Christiane Emilie. Duke Charles was an enterprising, entertaining man and when his father passed away, he inherited the leadership of the City of Mirow and Empire of Mecklenburg., where he ruled for a number of years. Duke Charles was educated at the University of Greifswald, one of the oldest universities in Germany, founded in 1456. He served as a Lieutenant Colonel in the Army of the Holy Roman Empire and was an accomplished musician who played the transverse flute and performed concerts in Switzerland, Italy, and France. His wife was Elizabeth Albertina of Saxe-Hildburghausen and together they had eight children, including Charlotte.

Duke Charles Louis Frederick, Charlotte's father[25]

Duke Charles's family descended from a tribe called the "Obotrites." They were a warlike, violent people who ruled Mecklenberg, Germany 700 years before Charlotte was born. [26] One of the early leaders in the region of Mecklenburg was Niklot, a warrior prince of the Obotrites. The chief occupations of the tribe were forestry, cattle-raising, hunting, and fishing. Their native religion was a pure worship of nature that was not connected to the one God, who is the principal religious icon of Christianity.

As an independent people, the Obotrites resisted Christianity for many centuries, until 900 A.D., when the Holy Roman Empire conquered them and took over the region of Mecklenburg. The German missionaries tied to the Holy Roman Empire worked to convert the Obotrites, and over time Christianity did spread throughout their culture. By the time Charlotte was born, Mecklenburg, Germany was a Christian backbone of the Holy Roman Empire and the descendants of the Obotrites were Christians. They held power in Germany, Italy and other parts of Europe for over 1,000 years.[27] The Lutheran Church was the primary Christian denomination in Mecklenburg, and Charlotte and her siblings were raised as Lutherans.

Charlotte's Mother

Charlotte's mother was Princess Elizabeth Albertina (1713-61). According to Mario de Valdes y Cocom, a PBS Frontline producer, Princess Albertina was descended from Margarita de Castro y Sousa, a noblewoman and descendant of a Moorish (African) branch of the Portuguese Royal House.[28] Mr. Cocom used genealogical records and archival material to trace Princess Albertina's ancestry to a thirteenth-century Portuguese ruler named Alfonso III, and his lover Madragana, whom Cocum states was a Moor.[29] There is some controversy about whether or not Madragana was a Moor but, there is no debate that Alfonso III warred against the Moors in Portugal, and defeated them. It was common during those days, for conquering warriors to mate with the women of defeated populations, and Madragana would have been in that category. Note: the English Oxford Dictionary defines Moor as, "A member of a Northwest African Muslim people of mixed Berber and Arab descent." [30] The Moors from Africa

were brown-skinned people who migrated from East Africa, Northern Africa, and the Middle East to parts of Europe. The Encyclopedia Britannica, defines "Moor" as "a Moroccan, or member of the Muslim population in the countries of Spain and Portugal. [31] Interestingly, history books about Spain, Portugal and other parts of Europe don't often mention the Moors as people of African descent, even though they came from North Africa and ruled Portugal and parts of Spain for centuries.[32]

Charlotte's Mother, Princess Elizabeth Albertina, Duchess of Mecklenburg-Strelitz (1713-61).

Portrait by Daniel Woge[33]

Cocom claims there are six different lines that trace Charlotte's genealogy to Margarita de Castro y Sousa, in a gene pool with Moorish blood, that was due to Royal inbreeding. Cocom believes that when Princess Albertina married Duke Charles, Charlotte's father, she handed down a Moorish heritage from her mixed race maternal ancestors Margarita de Castro y Sousa and Madragana, to her children and grandchildren, including her daughter Charlotte. [34] Princess Albertina's heritage is reinforced in a portrait by artist Daniel Woge, that shows her with features that reflect African or Moorish heritage. Readers can obtain information about Cocom's research into Charlotte's family at the PBS Frontline television production titled, "Blurred Racial Lines of Famous Families." Information about the television program is available at website:www.pbs.org/wgbh/pages/frontline/shows/secret/famous/ . Royalfamily.html

In 1752, when her husband Duke Charles died, Princess Albertina took over as "Regent" or official representative for her 14-year old son Duke Adolf Friedrich IV. The Duke was next in line to receive power from his father but, since he was too young to govern, his mother served as his representative until he became old enough to rule by himself. Charlotte and her siblings learned about governing as they watched their mother wield power and make important decisions on behalf of the House of Mecklenburg. They traveled with her to various cities in Germany on official business, as well as for medical and healing treatments. As Regent, Princess Albertina gained the respect of Royal Families in England, Prussia, Scandinavia, Scotland and France, including King George III's father and mother in England.

Mixed Race Heritage

When girls in Royal families in Germany and other parts of Europe, were selected as potential brides for arranged marriages, their heritage and ethnic backgrounds were researched by the families interested in them as potential brides for their sons. The backgrounds of parents, grandparents, places of birth and family origins of the girls considered for arranged marriages were studied to see if they were compatible with the family they were marrying into. In keeping with that tradition, Charlotte's background would have been investigated to determine if she was an appropriate wife for George III, heir to the throne of England. This would have included her mixed race heritage.

Family Background

Charlotte's Portrait on Cover of J.A. Rodgers Book, "Nature Knows No Color Line"

Mario de Valdes y Cocom, a Jesuit-educated man from Belize, historian of the African diaspora and researcher for the Public Broadcasting System, (PBS) became fascinated with Charlotte's heritage and researched it extensively. Cocom wrote, "With features as conspicuously Negroid as they were reputed to be by her contemporaries, it is no wonder that the black community, both in the U.S. and throughout the British Commonwealth rallied around pictures of Queen Charlotte for generations."[35]

Various authors and researchers pointed out the physiological traits that so obviously identified the mixed race ethnic strain of the young woman who at first glance, looks almost anomalous, portrayed as she usually is, in the sumptuous splendor of her coronation robes." [36] Although Cocom suggests that black communities rallied around Charlotte's picture and photos that knowledge did not transfer to contemporary black communities in America. Very few African American citizens are aware of Charlotte and her mixed-race heritage.

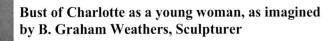

Bust of Charlotte as a young woman, as imagined by B. Graham Weathers, Sculpturer

In 1952, a noted, distinguished black historian named J.A. Rodgers featured a portrait of

CHAPTER TWO
Family Background

Charlotte painted by British-Irish artist Thomas Frye, on the cover of his book, Nature Knows No Color Line.[37] Inside the book, Rodger's displayed Charlotte's portrait on a page with the caption, "An Ancestress of George VI of England." Rodgers wrote, "Queen Charlotte Sophia, Consort of George III, and grandmother of Queen Victoria from a portrait by Thomas Frye (1719 – 1762). She was a German princess." Rodgers continued, "The evident Negro strain in Queen Charlotte Sophie consort of George III of England, who was a German princess, might be explained...see her portrait." In the book, Sex and Race, Volume 1, Rodgers wrote, "Charlotte Sophia...had the broad nostrils and heavy lips of the blond Negroid type."[38] Rodgers opinion about Charlotte is consistent with the conclusions drawn by Mario de Valdes y Cocom.

Throughout Charlotte's life members of the British Court and historians commented about her appearance. One noted English historian named Horace Walpole wrote about Charlotte in his letters, "...her nose very well, except the nostrils spreading too wide. The mouth has the same fault, but her teeth are good. She talks a great deal, and French tolerably." [39] Note: Walpole wrote a 498-page book titled Memoirs of the Reign of King George the Third but, in his book he did not refer to Queen Charlotte a single time. This is an example of how Charlotte was often treated as an invisible woman. Perhaps Walpole had trouble accepting and respecting Queen Charlotte because of her non-traditional appearance. Another observer in the Court named Baron Stockmar, the British Court Physician, commented in his 1760 autobiography that Charlotte had a "true mulatto face."[40] Mulatto is defined by Merriam Webster dictionary as a, "Person of mixed white/black ancestry."[41] Given these remarks it is obvious that there was chatter and speculation in the British Court and British society about Charlotte's heritage.

Another artist who portrayed his concept of Charlotte's facial appearance was sculpturer Dr. B. Graham Weathers, a North Carolina physician. Weathers traveled to England, in December 1994, to visit historic sites where Charlotte had lived in Germany and England, and to view portraits of her. He produced a rendition of Charlotte in a sculpture with his interpretation of what she would have looked in her mid-30's.[42] His sculpture of her facial features and thick hair shows that she would have qualified for the "one drop rule" used in the American colonies to define Black Americans. Note: per the Harvard Gazette, In the United States, the "one-drop rule" dates to a 1662 Virginia law on the treatment of mixed-race individuals. The legal definition of the one drop rule was upheld as recently as 1985, when a Louisiana court ruled that a woman with an African

American great-great-great-great-grandmother could not identify herself as "white" on her passport."[43] If Charlotte had been judged by the "one-drop rule" in America, she would have been classified as a mixed-race woman of Negro or black heritage. If she had lived in the American colonies during the 1700's, she could have been enslaved.

CHAPTER THREE
In Search of a Wife for George III

George III was born June 4, 1738, at Norfolk House, in St. James Square, London. He was the eldest son of Frederick, Prince of Wales, and Princess Augusta of Saxe-Gotha (aka Dowager Augusta). George III was the first King to be born on British soil and the first to use English as his first language. All prior British Kings were born in Germany, showing the close relationship between the British and the Germans.

George III was tall and handsome and a favorite among the ladies at Court. As a young boy, at the insistence of their father George III and his younger brother Edward were tutored in the arts and sciences. In addition to chemistry and physics, their lessons included astronomy, mathematics, French, Latin, history, music, geography, commerce, agriculture and constitutional law, along with sporting and social accomplishments such as dancing, fencing, and riding.

Portrait of King George III by Alan Ramsey[44]

Some historians claim George III was well read, smart and a good leader, while others say he was spoiled and slow to grow up. Yet, others historians complain that George III was a failure since he lost the American colonies during the American Revolutionary War. However, all agree that as he aged, he developed a serious illness that resulted in behavioral difficulties. But, despite his health difficulties George III reigned as King of England, for 57 years.

CHAPTER THREE
In Search of a Wife for King George III

Background of George III's Father

George III's father, Prince Frederick Lewis, Prince of Wales was born in Hanover, Germany, February 1, 1707. His father King George II and his mother Queen Caroline of Ansbach virtually abandoned him in Germany, for 14 years in the care of his grandparents. This abandonment caused Prince Frederick to develop a harsh personality. When his parents finally sent for him to move to England to live with them he was angry and rebellious. When he got to England, Prince Frederick demanded his father King George II give him a bigger allowance, but the King refused.

King George's III Father, Frederick Lewis, Prince of Wales[45]

As a young man, Prince Frederick took his fight for a bigger allowance to the British House of Commons and won. The open defiance of their son angered his mother, Queen Caroline and she was quoted as saying, "My dear first born is the greatest ass and the greatest liar, the greatest canaille (riff-raff or rabble), and the greatest beast in the whole world, and I most heartily wish he was out of it."[46] It was obvious the relationship between Prince Frederick and his parents was very strained. George III's personality had to have been affected by his father who was raised by such stressful parents. His father died from a burst abscess in his lungs when George III was only 22 years old. The bitterness in the family was confirmed when neither his father King George II, his mother Queen Caroline nor, any member of the Royal Family attended Prince Frederick's funeral. The tragedy of his father's death unexpectedly thrust George III into the role of King of England even though he was immature and not ready to rule. But, as heir to the throne George III had to become the King so, he learned to rely on his mother, grandfather and other court advisors for guidance and advice.[47]

CHAPTER THREE
In Search of a Wife for King George III

George III's Mother

George III's mother, the Dowager Augusta[48]

George III's mother was the Dowager Augusta. When his father died, she stepped in to act as his Regent and representative, until he was officially crowned as the King of England. Dowager Augusta had come to England from Germany, at the age of 16 for an arranged marriage with Prince Frederick Lewis, George III's father. As a young bride, she was awkward during her wedding ceremony, and was seen acting like a child and clutching a doll. Since Augusta only spoke German, she couldn't understand a word the court officials were saying at her wedding, until Prince Frederick's mother Queen Caroline of Ansbach started translating the ceremonial words from English to German.[49] After she married Prince Frederick, Augusta learned how to speak English and how to operate in the Royal Family. When she became a mature adult woman and mother of King George III and his siblings, she overcame her timidity and became strong and domineering. The Dowager Augusta was a force to be reckoned with in the Court.

George III's Siblings

As noted earlier, the Royal Family was full of stressful relationships. According to Stella Tillyard, author of "A Royal Affair: George III and His Troublesome Siblings," King George III didn't get along well with his brothers and sisters Edward, William, Henry, Augusta and Caroline Mathilde. His brothers hated public life and sought their privacy, while struggling to hide secret romances and avoid arranged marriages.[50] As a young man, George spent lots of time responding to scandals and outrageous behaviors of his siblings. He disapproved of his brothers having out-of-wedlock children and marrying women who weren't considered by his family to be nobility. In order to control his siblings, in 1772 King George III instituted the Royal Marriages Act, that mandated the King of England had the power to consent to marriages of any lineal descendant of his grandfather George II, with certain exceptions.[51] The Royal Marriage Act exists today and governs the behavior of the 21st Century Royal Family of England.

Rumors about George III's First Love

In the mid-1700's a rumor circulated that King George III was romantically involved with a Quaker woman named Hannah Lightfoot, (October 12, 1730 – December 1759). The story goes that Hannah, known as the *"Fair Quaker"* was 23 years old and unhappily married to a grocer named Isaac Axford. George III reportedly met Hannah at a social gathering when he was 15, and they fell in love.

Per rumors, George III helped Hannah escape from her marriage to Isaac and hid her away for several years. Some claimed Hannah and George III had two or three children during their secret relationship and while there was no proof, the

rumor was a major source of gossip during the mid-1700's, and several books were written about their alleged relationship.[52] It is likely the gossip about George III and Hannah contributed to the urgency of the Royal Family wanting to get George III married to someone who would be considered acceptable as the future Queen of England. Author Mary Pendered claims that several years after the 1761 coronation wedding of George III and Charlotte reports surfaced that Hannah Lightfoot disappeared or, died from unknown causes. In later years, some individuals came forth to claim they were the children of King George III and Hannah, but no one believed them and they did not receive any inheritance from his estate.[53]

Hannah Lightfoot, painted by Joshua Reynolds, First President Royal Academy of Arts[54]

A Bride for King George III

When George III was 22, his grandfather George II and mother Dowager Augusta started searching throughout Europe for a bride so, he could start a family of future heirs to the throne.[55] At first, several young, single women were

In Search of a Wife for King George III

considered including Princess Sophie Caroline of Brunswick-Wolfenbuttel; 14-year old Frederica Louise of Saxe-Gotha; and Lady Sarah Lennox, daughter of the Duke of Richmond. George III had a crush on Lady Sarah but, his mother Dowager Augusta didn't like Sarah so, she was eliminated as a potential bride.

It was tough for George III's family to reach a decision about a bride since his mother and grandfather disagreed about who would be the best choice. His grandfather wanted him to marry a young lady from the Court of Frederick the Great, since he thought an alliance with Prussia would strengthen the British Empire. However, his mother despised Frederick the Great for his role in the

Seven Years War so, she took all potential brides from Prussia off the list of eligible candidates. Biographer Thomas Williams wrote, "The late King (George II) wished his grandson (George III) to marry a niece of the King of Prussia (Frederick the Great) but, the Prince's mother, the Princess Dowager of Wales, was averse to an alliance with that Court...her reason for this was said to be her aversion to the character of Frederick the Great, whom she considered as an unprincipled infidel who fought his own battles at England's expense..."[56]

Duke Earl Bute, who oversaw selection of Charlotte, portrait by Sir Joshua Reynolds, 1773[57]

As the Royal Family searched across Europe for a bride for King George III, Princess Sophia Charlotte of Mecklenburg Strelitz's name came up as a young woman to consider. George III's mother Dowager Augusta had heard about the letter Charlotte had sent to Frederick the Great to complain about his role in the Seven Years War, and she was impressed. The more Dowager Augusta and his grandfather King George II learned about Charlotte, the more interested they became. Since no one at the court had seen or met Princess Charlotte, the Dowager Augusta asked her friend The Right Honorable John Stuart, 3rd Earl of Bute (Duke Bute) to send a representative to Mecklenburg, Germany to investigate her. If after his investigation, Duke Bute found Charlotte to be a suitable candidate for George III, and if Dowager Augusta and George III approved, Duke Bute would negotiate a marriage agreement with Charlotte's

In Search of a Wife for King George III

family. Duke Bute personally handled this confidential task because he was a close friend of Dowager Augusta, a mentor to George III and a trusted ally.

Duke Bute asked Colonel David Graeme, a soldier he trusted, to go to Mirow, Germany, to meet with Charlotte's family. The Colonel left immediately carrying a "Proposal of Marriage" letter from Dowager Augusta to Charlotte's mother, Princess Elizabeth Albertina. The letter was to be presented after Colonel Graeme interviewed Charlotte and determined that her looks, personality, and intelligence made her suitable to be George III's wife, and the future Queen of England.

Charlotte's brother, Duke Adolph Frederick IV, negotiated the marriage[58]

Duke Bute and Dowager Augusta had heard good reports about Charlotte's mother, the Princess Albertina and the Mecklenburg family. They heard that after her husband's death, Princess Elizabeth Albertina had done a good job as "Regent" for her son Duke Adolf Friedrich IV. They knew Princess Albertina was the key decision-maker in Mecklenburg-Strelitz, until her son Adolf was old enough to become the leader in his own right.[59] When Duke Bute and Dowager Augusta sent Colonel Graeme to Mirow to investigate the potential of an arranged marriage with Charlotte, her brother Duke Adolph was firmly in charge of the Mecklenburg Family affairs, and was prepared to negotiate with Colonel Graeme.

Colonel Graeme traveled to Germany to meet with Princess Albertina, Charlotte and Adolph. However, when he arrived at the City of Mirow, he learned Charlotte and her mother had gone to a spa at Bad Prymont, in Hanover, Germany. Bad Prymont was a popular place for aristocrats to go for healing, and Princess Albertina went there regularly. Bad Prymont was also a central meeting place for the Quaker community.[60] Note: during the 1700's and 1800's the Quakers were the backbone of the anti-slavery Abolitionist movement in England, and the world. It is likely that Princess Albertina and Charlotte had Quaker friends they met, during their frequent visits to Bad Prymont.

Sadly, Princess Albertina was very ill so, Charlotte and her siblings had to take her to the spa in Bad Prymont for special healing treatments, in the mineral

In Search of a Wife for King George III

waters. Soon it became obvious that Princess Albertina's illness was terminal. When Colonel Graeme arrived in Mirow and learned that Charlotte and her mother were in Bad Prymont, he immediately went to Bad Prymont to see them. Although she was very ill, Princess Albertina met with the Colonel and discussed the possible marriage proposal from George III. After their meeting, Princess Albertina asked Charlotte's brother, Duke Adolf Friedrich IV, to handle any follow-up, in the event a marriage proposal was offered for his sister's hand in marriage. And, of course the Duke was prepared to respond to any proposal, for an arranged marriage with George III.

Colonel Graeme was very impressed with Charlotte's family, and enjoyed meeting Charlotte and her mother. After their meeting, he sent a message to Dowager Augusta and Earl Bute in Britain, that he liked Charlotte's personality, admired her caretaking of her mother, and thought her sturdy build would make her a good mother and child bearer. When Colonel Graeme left Bad Prymont and went back to Mirow, he met with Duke Adolf Frederick IV, who greeted him with every honor the small Court of Mirow could provide. Duke Adolf knew the stakes were high with the prospect of his sister marrying George III, the King of England. Adolf knew if Charlotte married into the British Royal Family, it would establish a powerful alliance for the House of Mecklenburg-Strelitz, and their colleagues and relatives.

When Colonel Graeme met with Duke Adolf he posed questions about Charlotte's religious upbringing. Charlotte's religious affiliation was important because it was mandatory that all Queens of England belonged to the Anglican Church. Graeme knew that the Mecklenburg Family was a leading supporter of the Catholic Holy Roman Empire in Germany so, he wanted to know if the family was Roman Catholic. If Charlotte was Catholic it would automatically disqualify her from marrying George III and being the Queen of England, since the Anglicans and Catholics were enemies. Duke Adolf was happy to explain to Colonel Graeme that although his family supported the Holy Roman Empire, they belonged to the Lutheran Church, and that Charlotte was a Christian, not a Catholic. When Colonel Graeme heard Charlotte was Lutheran he could confidently assure the Dowager Augusta, George III's grandfather, and the British Parliament that Charlotte's loyalties and religious affiliations would not undermine the throne of England. This was very important.

Duke Adolph pledged under the terms of the marriage contract that his sister Charlotte would join the Anglican Church, and be married under Anglican religious rites. He also pledged that Charlotte would not involve herself in British

In Search of a Wife for King George III

politics. During their meeting, Colonel Graeme received favorable answers to all of his concerns and following the meeting he sent a letter to England, by horseback messenger to recommend the marriage should proceed. It took a few days for the letter to be received by Duke Bute, and for the Duke to present his recommendation to the Royal Family that Charlotte was a suitable bride for George III. Still in Mirow, Colonel Graeme waited for approval from the Royal Family and when he received it he presented Duke Adolph with the marriage proposal letter, and waited for an official response from Charlotte's family.

Since this was an arranged marriage between the leaders of the British Royal family and the Mecklenburg Royal Family, the bride-to-be had very little to say about the decision. As was the custom, Charlotte was required to go along with the wishes of her family, regarding who she would marry. The only person who could have vetoed the marriage was Princess Albertina, Charlotte's mother. And, even though Princess Albertina was on her death bed, she was very pleased about the marriage proposal for her beloved daughter. She told her son to speak on her behalf when he responded to Dowager Augusta's letter and to inform the British Royal family that the Family of Mecklenburg accepted the offer of marriage for Charlotte.[61] Unfortunately, soon after the complicated marriage negotiations were completed, Princess Albertina died, with her beloved daughter Charlotte, son Adolph and her other children by her side. It was very sad that Princess Elizabeth Albertina did not get to see her daughter become the Queen of England.

It had to be very traumatic for Charlotte to lose her mother at the same time she was being asked to move to England, to marry King George III. As a compassionate young woman with strong feelings about the people she loved and her family, it was tough to leave but, since her family had made the decision for her to marry King George III she was required to comply. Before leaving Mirow, Charlotte helped with her mother's funeral arrangements and stood with the family at the funeral service. She was present when her mother was buried at the family cemetery, behind Mirow Castle and one can only imaging the grieving she felt.

The British Royal family made it clear through Colonel Graeme that they were anxious for Charlotte to travel to England, as soon as possible for the wedding to George III. Charlotte knew it was her mother's last wish that she marry George III, so she did what was necessary and prepared to leave her hometown. Right in the middle of participating in the funeral arrangements for

CHAPTER THREE
In Search of a Wife for King George III

her mother, Charlotte had to pack her belongings and prepare to leave. She didn't know that she would never see her childhood home again.

CHAPTER FOUR
The Coronation

After secret meetings at the Royal Court were held and agreements were reached with Charlotte's family, regarding the arranged marriage of Charlotte to King George III, members in the King's court were finally told that King George III was getting married. They were surprised to hear about plans for George III to get married immediately and arrangements were quickly made. Lord Harcourt, one of the Court Officials, was appointed Ambassador to Mecklenburg to formally request Princess Charlotte's hand in marriage, and to escort her back to England.[62] Harcourt led a party of well-dressed ladies and a procession of grand carriages to transport Charlotte and her companions, for the three-day trip from Mecklenburg, through Hanover, Germany, to the coastal city of Stade, and then to England.

Royal Yacht of Caroline, Renamed HMY Royal Yacht Charlotte[63]

The escort party that came from England to escort Charlotte was very fancy, festive, colorful and dramatic. A Royal procession traveled the roads of Mecklenburg and drew thousands of curious people onto the streets in Mirow, Mecklenburg, and in adjoining cities and towns. The citizens of Germany wanted to extend their condolences to Charlotte at the loss of her beloved mother, Princess Elizabeth Albertina, whom they loved and knew well. At the same time, they wanted to extend their congratulations to Charlotte, daughter of the Royal Mecklenburg family who was going to marry King George III and to become the Queen of England.

CHAPTER FOUR
The Coronation

On August 28, 1761, Charlotte and her escorts reached the City of Stade where they boarded a splendidly appointed yacht. King George III renamed the yacht for Charlotte as the "HMY Royal Charlotte." The escort party and the bride-to-be boarded the four yachts that were moored at the port town of Cuxhaven, in the northern Hanoverian Region, at the Elbe River. Lord Hardwicke, the British Navy Commander, and a crew of 40 people joined the Royal staff on the yachts to set sail to the North Sea. The yacht captain was Lord Anson, of the Royal Navy, who led the HMY Royal Charlotte, that was outfitted with 24 guns and escorted by 6 warships.[64] Crowds of well-wishers met the yachts at every port, to celebrate the upcoming union of Charlotte and King George III.

Portrait of Charlotte by Allan Ramsay

During the voyage to England, the ocean was rough and the yachts struggled through several terrible storms. They were blown to the Norwegian coast three times. Finally, after nine days they arrived in Harwich, a town in Essex, England. [65] The storms were so terrible that the staff and five ladies-in-waiting got sea sick, and were miserable. However, Charlotte maintained her composure and comforted the crew and ladies-in-waiting by singing and playing her harpsichord. Even though she couldn't speak English, Charlotte knew the British national anthem "God Save the King" and sang it to the crew. Her charming personality impressed the British staff so much that when they arrived in England, they had nothing but enthusiastic praise for her sea-worthiness, talent, and graciousness.

When Charlotte arrived in England she was taken immediately to St. James Palace to meet her fiancé King George III. She was 17 years old and he was 23. At their first arkward meeting, King George III and members of the Court were surprised at her mixed-race appearance. However, the personalities of Charlotte and George III instantly sparked. Since George's grandfather and the Dowager Augusta wanted them to get married immediately, a private marriage ceremony was hurriedly put together and on September 8, 1761, the day after Charlotte arrived in England, they were married at the Chapel Royal, at St. James

CHAPTER FOUR
The Coronation

Palace. Following the private ceremony, the Court started planning for the official Coronation to take place two weeks later, on September 22, 1761. The official Coronation would take place at Westminster Abbey Church and officially crown George III as King of Great Britain and Ireland, and anoint Charlotte, as his Queen.

Life was moving fast for Charlotte. Within one month the she had participated in the funeral of her mother; traveled in a procession of carriages for miles through Germany to the coastal city of Stade; responded to crowds of people cheering her on and wishing her sympathy; cruised in a stormy yacht trip to get to England; consoled the seasick crew with music and singing; married a man she didn't know; and was told she would be married a second time at an official Royal Coronation attended by European dignitaries. In addition, Charlotte was informed that within 30 days she would be crowned Queen of England and Ireland. Fortunately, her schooling and her mother had prepared her well so she didn't lose her temper, become hysterical or, otherwise embarrass herself and her family. From all accounts, Sophia Charlotte of Mecklenburg-Strelitz, daughter of Duke Charles Louis Frederick and Duchess Elizabeth Albertina rose to the occasion and handled the complex dynamics she was facing, with grace and dignity.

Coronation and Wedding

On September 22, 1761, the official Coronation was held to publicly celebrate the marriage of George III and Charlotte. The grand event was held at Westminister Abbey, a church established in the 1040's in London, England. As the Coronation approached, people were so excited that no one could think or talk about anything else. Crowds filled the streets and there were reports of collisions of horse-drawn carriages, as they raced to reach Westminster Abbey on Coronation day.

Site of Coronation at Westminster Abbey, in London England[66]

CHAPTER FOUR
The Coronation

George III and Charlotte rode to Westminster Hall separately in elegantly decorated sedan chairs. They walked into the Hall in grand, formal attire and were heralded by many dignitaries from around the world. Charlotte walked down the aisle under a canopy of shining gold cloth accompanied by a procession of ladies-in-waiting, holding her train. Her gown was described as silver embroidered with gold, over a tissue petticoat with a diamond stomacher, velvet sleeves, diamonds and pearls big as cherries. Over her dress, she wore a velvet surcoat and mantel with ermine and lace, while she carefully carried a beautiful fan made of mother of pearl, emeralds, rubies and diamonds. [67]

Silver bells tinkled at each corner of the vast rooms as she and King George III stood before Thomas Secker, Archbishop of Canterbury, who led the ceremony. It must have been hard for Charlotte to believe that only two weeks earlier she had been in her home, in the castle at Moritz, Mecklenburg-Strelitz and that she was now preparing to become the Queen of England.

Queen Charlotte in Coronation State gown by artist Allan Ramsay, 1761 [68]

The event at Westminster Abbey was a combined wedding ceremony and Coronation for George III to officially become King. It was exciting for everyone who was there including George III's friends, schoolmates and playmates. Unfortunately, since Charlotte was so far from home she didn't have the pleasure of having her brothers, sisters and friends at the wedding so, it was a lonely experience for her. The newly crowned Queen was introduced to her new Royal Family and met many of the people she would interact with for the rest of her life. The website 'History Today' reports, "When the crown was placed on George's head a huge cheer went up from the boys of Westminster School and the rest of the congregation. And, when the Archbishop of Canterbury climbed into the pulpit to deliver his sermon, the congregation took the opportunity to listen, as they ate huge supplies of cold meat and pies and drank plenty of wine they had brought with them. Platters of food were also handed around by servants, with a noisy clattering of plates, glasses, and cutlery.[69]

The Coronation

Coronation Banquet of George III and Queen Charlotte, in Westminster Hall, in 1761 by R. Wilkinson

Following the formal ceremony, guests enjoyed an expansive banquet of 100 different dishes on elaborate platters, along with massive displays of foliage and flowers, that decorated the banquet halls of St. James Palace. King George III and Queen Charlotte received their dinners on gold plates with elaborate silverware and crystal. Twenty dozen flasks of champagne and 50 dozen of red port wine were served to the guests. Four master chefs prepared the delicious meals and according to a painting by R. Wilkerson, there were rows and rows of guests who took part in the regal pageantry. [70]

Some of the gifts presented to the Royal couple have survived for hundreds of years and are stored in Royal Collections around the world. For example, a bronze medal featuring Queen Charlotte was minted in 1761, by

Johann Lorenz Natter, an engraver at the English Royal Mint. The medal was stored for many years in the United States, in the Numismatic archives of Yale University Library, New Haven, Connecticut. The coin is stored in the collection at Yale University Art Library but, is not on public view. [71]

Coronation Medal of Queen Charlotte, Engraver: Johann Lorenz Natter, 1705 – 1763

CHAPTER FOUR
The Coronation

The actual crown Charlotte wore at the Coronation was not preserved. However, various artists sketched pictures of a gold crown that showed a cross at the top symbolizing the Christian faith of England.

Sketch of crown worn by Queen Charlotte[72]

Poetic Tribute to Queen Charlotte

Poem About Queen Charlotte Written at the Time of Her Wedding to George III

Descended from the warlike Vandal race,

She still preserves that title in her face.

Tho' shone their triumphs o'er Numidia's plain,

And Alusian fields their name retain;

They but subdued the southern world with arms,

She conquers still with her triumphant charms,

O! born for rule, - to whose victorious brow

The greatest monarch of the north must bow.

Anonymous Author, 1761

CHAPTER FOUR
The Coronation

When George III and Charlotte got married an unknown poet wrote a poem about her. The poem made creative references that described the author's perception of Charlotte being descended from a country in Africa. The poet wrote that Charlotte was, "Descended from the warlike Vandal race, she still preserves that title in her face." This would suggest that Charlotte had a trace of African culture in her appearance—a observation shared by historians quoted in this book. Note: the Vandals were an East Germanic tribe of warriors who in 100AD established a kingdom in North Africa."[73] The poet also mentioned "Numidia" a country in North Africa, near the Mediterranean Sea, populated by brown-skinned people. The poem refers to "Alusian Fields," an area on the Alusian Islands in the arctic region of Alaska, that had been explored by Russians who found people with brown-skinned appearances, similar to Charlotte's. [74]

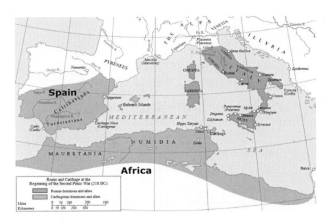

Map showing Numidia, in North Africa

Post-Wedding Visit with Quakers

Author Olwen Hedley reports, after the Coronation ceremony newly crowned King George III and his wife Queen Charlotte went to visit a Quaker family, who lived in London. The newlyweds spent four private hours with the family, an indication that they felt comfortable with them. Hedley reports a quote from one of the Quaker guests who attended the celebration, "…Hearts filled with mingled astonishment and ecstasy."[75]

The Quakers, also known as the Religious Society of Friends, were founded in England in the 1600's by George Fox (1624-1691), a nonconformist religious reformer who left the Anglican Church.[76] It is interesting to note that over the years King George III and Queen Charlotte had connections with Quakers in England, Germany and in the American colonies. When she was alive, Charlotte's mother, the Princess Elizabeth Albertina, regularly visited the town of Bad Prymont, Germany—a Quaker headquarters—for medical and mineral health treatments. Also, it was rumored that George III had an intimate relationship with Hannah Lightfoot, a young Quaker woman. For whatever reason, Quakers played a significant role in Charlotte's life and the importance of Quakers increased as she became older.

Three Wedding Ceremonies

Queen Charlotte and King George III had three marriage ceremonies. First, they were married the day after her arrival to London in a hasty private ceremony. Several weeks later they had the elaborate wedding at Westminster Abbey. However, there was one other marriage ceremony. Author William Thoms wrote in his book, "Queen Charlotte and Chevalier D'EON," that in 1765, a few years after their Coronation Wedding, Charlotte insisted King George III renew his marriage vows to her in a third ceremony at Kew Gardens, at one of their residences. This ceremony was performed by Dr. Wilmot, the king's physician. Perhaps this third wedding ceremony was prompted by Charlotte hearing about the Hannah Lightfoot rumors and wanting to be reassured that George III loved her. Or, another reason may have been that Charlotte dreamed of getting married in a garden setting, rather than an official, pompous environment like the Westminster Coronation, and the King indulged her. In any event, Edward the King's brother, attended all three of the marriage ceremonies.[77]

King George III, Marriage and Illness

From most accounts, King George III and Charlotte had a good marriage for most of the 57 years they were together. However, periodically their happiness was severely challenged by an illness that King George III developed that was believed to be mental illness but, was later diagnosed as a condition known as porphyria. The acute condition of porphyria is a genetic disease and causes numerous symptoms including severe abdominal pain, swelling of the abdomen, constipation, diarrhea, vomiting, insomnia, seizures, and mental changes, such as confusion, hallucinations, disorientation or paranoia and even paralysis.[78]

CHAPTER FOUR
The Coronation

George III became very sick during his middle to older years and displayed behaviors that were interpreted to be mental illness. Queen Charlotte and his Court staff tried to hide his condition from the public but, it eventually came out. His periodic illness created a traumatic situation since it was very severe when it hit. King George III could be well for a while and then he would lapse into mental confusion and would have to be physically restrained. He was often locked in a room. Charlotte's skills were tested as she worked with his doctors to be a caregiver for her husband.

The King's mental illness has been discussed for centuries. A film called, 'Madness of King George" was produced in America and became the primary media source of information that created the historic image of King George III and Queen Charlotte.[79] The film showed incidents where the King acted unstable and had to be restrained by his doctors and staff. However, none of Charlotte's personal talents and qualities were shown in the film, and the film undoubtedly embarrassed the British people and the Royal Family. The film contributed to Charlotte's hidden image and invisibility in history.

At the Science Museum in England, there is an envelope containing hair taken from George III's head after his death. An analysis found the hair to be laden with arsenic, at a concentration over 300 times that is considered toxic. Arsenic is a well-known poison that can trigger porphyria. It is possible that the King might have taken the poison accidently when he was given certain medicines, like 'James Powders,' a common medicine in England during his lifetime. [80] Or, it may be that King George III actually suffered from a form of mental illness.

CHAPTER FIVE

Royal Residences

King George III and Queen Charlotte owned several residences in England, and outside of London, including St. James Palace, Buckingham Palace, Windsor Palace, Richmond Lodge and Frogmore. Some of their palaces were used to receive foreign dignitaries, while others were used as weekend retreats for them and their children. The Royal family enjoyed the grounds, gardens and brightly shining stars at the retreats outside of London. Over the years, their growing family of 15 children, plus grandparents and staff needed lots of space to entertain, play games, garden, and engage in music and sports.

St. James Palace

For the first year of their marriage, Charlotte and George III lived at St. James Palace, in London. But, after a short time King George found the formal Tudor architecture at the palace to be too restrictive for his growing family, so he investigated other places, where they could be more comfortable. After they moved, they continued to use St James Palace for formal occasions and public meetings but, most of the time they lived at their other homes.

St. James Palace, England
Buckingham Palace

In 1761, King George III bought Buckingham House for Queen Charlotte to use as a second official residence, and as a second location for official Court functions. In the 21st century, Buckingham House is still occupied by the Royal Family, and is known as Buckingham Palace. Buckingham House became known as the "Queen's House" and 14 of King George III and Queen Charlotte's 15 children were born there. [81] In 1762, King George retained architect Sir William

Chambers (1726-1796), to re-design the palace, and Chambers transformed it into the extraordinary Royal residence it is today.

**Buckingham Palace—
the Queen's House,
purchased by King
George in 1761**

Richmond Lodge: The Original White House

When King George III inherited property from his father Prince Frederick, he got a place called Richmond Lodge, where George lived as a bachelor. After about a year of being married to Charlotte, they starting using Richmond Lodge, as one of their second homes. King George's father, Prince Frederick of Wales, had rented Richmond Lodge in 1731 and the lodge was known as "His Royal Highness House at Kew." When Prince Frederick of Wales originally purchased Richmond Lodge he remodeled it and painted it white, and it became known as the "White House."

The term "White House" continued to be used to describe Richmond Lodge. Many people believe the name "White House" originated as a description of the presidential mansion on Pennsylvania Avenue, in Washington, D.C. but, the name "White House" started with Prince Frederick of Wales. Later afer King George III married Charlotte the country "White House" was a place where Charlotte taught her children farming, gardening, cricket and football and where they had many picnics. King George's parents Prince Frederick and the Dowager Augusta also started the famous Kew Gardens, at Richmond Lodge. Historically, the Dowager Augusta was the first woman to live in an official residence known as the "White House," and Queen Charlotte was the second.

Royal Residences

King George III's father, The Prince Frederick of Wales' bought the White House at Kew John Rocue's map *A New Plan of Richmond Garden* (1748)

Queen Charlotte's Cottage

A one-story building at the southwest end of Richmond Lodge came to be known as Queen Charlotte's Cottage. Since King George III and Queen Charlotte disliked the pomp and glamor of official Court life, they used Richmond Lodge as a retreat from Buckingham Palace, and also lived in the large and formal "White House" next door to Lodge. Queen Charlotte's Cottage became their real home and was the place where the family relaxed and studied. They enjoyed astronomy observatories that King George had built, and creatively designed buildings that included a Chinese-style aviary with a small flowerbed and a pond well-stocked with goldfish. Queen Charlotte developed her decorator skills when

she designed the cottage and she became known for her style and appreciation for architecture and design. In August 1774, a London Magazine wrote, "The Queen's cottage in the shade of the garden is a pretty retreat: the furniture is all English prints of elegance and humor. The design is said to be Her Majesty's." [82]

The Queen's Cottage at Richmond Lodge[83]

CHAPTER FIVE
Royal Residences

Kew Gardens

In the 1760's when King George III and Queen Charlotte moved to Richmond Lodge, they found the Kew Gardens that his parents had started, to be a perfect retreat. The Kew gardens started as 300 acres, located in the London Borough of Richmond, on the Thames River. The gardens became a location where botanists and explorers could store specimens from remote locations and exchange expertise and knowledge about plants that were foreign to England.[84] Currently known as the Royal Botanic Gardens at Kew, the gardens grow more species than any other garden in the world, and are a UNESCO World Heritage Site. The Kew Gardens are a worldwide botany research site and contain glasshouses and galleries that are available for tourists.

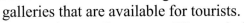

King George III admired architectural design and worked with a variety of architects to decorate his estates with innovative new buildings. One of the memorable buildings in the Kew Gardens is a 10-story pagoda, based on Asian architecture, built by his favorite architect Sir William Chambers, a man from Scotland who traveled regularly to China and India. Today, Chambers is regarded as one of the two greatest architects of late eighteenth-century Britain. He designed more than 25 buildings for the Royal Gardens, including the Pagoda that is decorated with 80 dragons, each carved from wood and gilded with real gold.

Pagoda at Kew Gardens designed by Sir William Chambers[85]

Royal Residences

New Menagerie

Next to the Queen's Cottage was a collection of rare animals called the "New Managerie." It was a colorful oval ring of pheasant pens at the end of a paddock, including fish, birds with colorful plumage, cattle, and even tigers. The New Menagerie was home to exotic creatures from the furthest reaches of the British Empire, including a pair of black swans and buffaloes. The first kangaroos

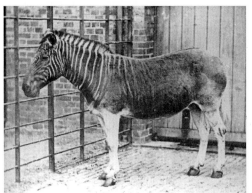

who arrived in England, were successfully bred at the New Menagerie. King George III and Queen Charlotte loved this exotic zoo and kept several of a breed of animal known as the quagga. The quagga was similar to zebras but, is now extinct. [86] Today, throughout the menagerie, there are ornamental animals displayed, in the memory of the actual animals that once lived there.

Rare Quagga at the New Managerie, photo by Frederick York and Frank Haes, 1870[87]

Windsor Castle

Windsor Castle was another part-time home of the Royal Family. It is one of the oldest and largest Royal residences in Europe, located about 40 miles southeast of London, in the county of Berkshire. This is an area with a long history of sheep farming. In contemporary times, there are annual sheep fairs held in the town of East Ilsley where the River Thames runs along Berkshire's northeast border. The area is a scenic waterway, mainly used for boating, leisure craft, and pleasure trips.

Royal Residences

Windsor Castle, Berkshire County

When she was at Windsor Castle, Queen Charlotte and her children enjoyed participating in the local traditions of the Berkshire community. One of the favorite traditions in Berkshire was called "Swan Upping." This was a  tradition of rounding up and counting local swans on the River Thames. Swan Upping dated back to the days when swans were an important food source for Royalty at banquets and feasts. Although swans are no longer eaten by Royalty, there is still an annual "Swan Upping" event where the swans are counted and their health is evaluated. The goal is to preserve the swans who still swim on the River Thames.[88]

Windsor Castle's lavish, early 19th-century state apartments are architecturally significant and are decorated with paintings done by such famous artists as Rembrandt, Rubens, and Canaletto.[89] The artistic flavor that King George III and Queen Charlotte established at Windsor Castle, led to artistic creations in later generations. For example, in the 1920's a doll house was set-up at Windsor Castle, called, "Queen Mary's Dolls' House." This Doll House was built for Queen Mary, one of Charlotte's great-granddaughters, by a leading British architect named Sir Edwin Lutyens, between 1921 and 1924. Queen Mary's Doll House is the largest, most famous doll house in the world, filled with thousands of objects made by leading artists, designers and craftsmen. The Doll House even includes electricity, running hot and cold water and flushing lavatories.[90] Queen Charlotte would have loved her great-granddaughter's Doll House.

Windsor Castle also includes the 15th-century St. George's Chapel, a church where Queen Charlotte and her family worshiped. St. Georges Chapel is the headquarters of the famous Royal organization known as 'Order of the Garter,' a fraternity of kings and princes that many male members of the Royal

Royal Residences

Family still belong to.[91] St. George's Chapel was the location of many weddings of the children, grandchildren and great-grandchildren of King George III and Queen Charlotte and many of the Royal Family members are buried there.

Frogmore at Windsor

In 1792, George III bought another new house for Queen Charlotte, within the confines of the Windsor Estate that adjoined the Kew Gardens. The new house was called Frogmore and was purchased after 30 years of marriage. Frogmore was another country retreat for the aging Queen and her married daughters. It provided them with a place to pursue their interests in reading, painting, drawing, needlework and japanning—the art of lacquering wood. They also botanized in the gardens and engaged in the study of plants. When she moved into Frogmore Queen Charlotte reportedly said, "I mean for this place to furnish me with fresh amusements every day." [92]

Frogmore, country retreat in 1790's

Charlotte personally selected artists to decorate the rooms at Frogmore. One of her favorite choices was Mary Moser (1744-1819), a renowned 18th-century flower painter who decorated one of Frogmore's principal rooms to resemble an arbor open to the skies. Mary Moser had been trained in the arts by her father, George Michael Moser, one of King George III's art teachers. Her father had to train her because women were barred from painting directly from live subjects.

Royal Residences

Painted Flowers, by Mary Moser, 1780[93]

Queen Charlotte intuitively understood that women in the workforce needed support from the Royal Family to be able to expand their talents and to achieve in their field of choice. Her support of Mary Moser enabled Mary to achieve recognition and fame as a decorator during the 1790s, which was unusual for a woman decorator. When the Queen commissioned Mary to design a complex floral decorative scheme for Frogmore House, it was applauded as excellent design work. The Queen also employed Mary to be a drawing teacher for her daughters and under her training, Charlotte's third daughter Princess Elizabeth became an accomplished artist.[94] Mary Moser inspired Elizabeth to paint the "Cross Gallery" at Frogmore with garlands that spanned the entire breadth of the House. Queen Charlotte advocated on behalf of women and girls and applauded their achievements.

CHAPTER SIX
Abolitionist & Advocate

Queen Charlotte could have been like many Royal family members who focused only on entertaining themselves, their families, musical concerts, gardens and entertainment. However, Charlotte was different because she had a social consciousness that was formed when she was a young girl and she was genuinely concerned about the welfare of others. Her awareness of human rights was particularly important since Charlotte lived during the time when the brutal, inhumane and highly profitable Trans-Atlantic slave trade was going on and millions of people of African heritage, were being sold into slavery.

The African slave trade began in the 1400's and for centuries was conducted by Britain, Netherlands, Portugal, Spain and France, in collaboration with the colonies in the New World, in North and South America. [95] Queen Charlotte knew there were Black people enslaved in England, since they were enslaved by the aristocratic class, who were close to the Royal Court. She also knew that British traders were kidnapping defenseless, people and transporting them to foreign lands where they were forced them into a lifetime of bondage and slavery. She had to hear about enslaved African people locked in chains in the bottoms of ships, with little food and no sanitation who were transported across the Atlantic Ocean, and purchased.

Since Queen Charlotte was an avid reader who interacted with world leaders, she was able to represent her husband when he was ill, behind the scenes with leaders in the British Parliament. She knew the British owned many of the slave ships that were trading products for live people, including knives, guns, ammunition, cotton cloth, tools, brass dishes, sugar, rice, tobacco, indigo, and rum. And, while there are no records that indicate King George III and Charlotte personally owned slaves or, had slaves at any of their residences, it is important to ask what did King George III and Queen Charlotte do about the slave trade? Did they support it, oppose it or ignore it?

Fortunately, history shows that Queen Charlotte joined the struggle and opposed the slave trade through personal relationships with Abolitionists, who actively advocated against slavery in the British Parliament. She regularly corresponded with Quaker Abolitionists in England, and North America and worked behind the scenes to abolish slavery in England.

Friends with Leading Abolitionists

Abolitionist Granville Sharp[96]

One close friend of King George III and Queen Charlotte was Granville Sharp (1735-1813), a leader of the "Anti-Saccharine (sugar) Campaign." The Queen and King met regularly with Granville Sharp in formal and informal settings. Since Sharp and his family were musicians the Royal family invited them to perform concerts at Kew Gardens. The concerts provided informal opportunities for them to strategize opposition to slavery, within the British Parliament. In 1787, Sharp formed the 'Society for Effecting the Abolition of the Slave Trade,' to fight on behalf of enslaved blacks, who were kidnapped, enslaved and sold to plantations in the American colonies, and the West Indies. Sharp's movement against sugar was the world's first recorded economic boycott. Sharp and his allies mounted public appeals and solicited donations to fund organized boycotts of West Indian sugar. Granville Sharp's "Anti-Saccharine Campaign"[97] opposed the trade of black men and women in exchange for sugar cane and although it took several decades, his fierce opposition of the slave trade in the British Parliament, contributed to the final abolishment of slavery. Sharp also helped establish colonies for free blacks to move to Sierra Leone, in West Africa, to establish free communities. Queen Charlotte openly supported Sharp's Anti-Saccharine protest.

In 1772, Sharp represented a case about slavery on English soil, that was a landmark case known as *Somersett's Case*. This ruling was about an enslaved black man named James Somersett, who was the property of a Boston customs official, and brought to England. After two years he escaped, but was recaptured and was forced onto a ship bound for Jamaica. With help from Granville Sharpe, Chief Justice Lord Mansfield, ordered the Captain of the ship on which Somerset was incarcerated, to produce Somersett before a court. Mansfield ruled in 1772 that 'no master ever was allowed here (England) to take a slave by force to be sold abroad because he deserted from his service...therefore the man must be discharged'. [98] And so James Somersett won his freedom and slavery was abolished on British soil. However, although slavery was declared illegal in

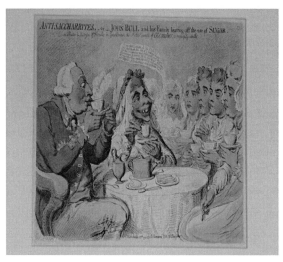

England in 1772, it remained legal in most of the British Empire for several more decades and was legal in the American colonies for almost another hundred years until the Civil War. Sharp also assisted blacks who escaped slavery, to establish a free settlement in Sierra Leone. [99]

Satirical Anti-Slavery/Anti-Saccharrites Cartoon Featuring King George III and Queen Charlotte, Published March 27, 1792, by H.H. Humphrey, N18[100]

One item of evidence that indicates Queen Charlotte opposed slavery was shown in 1792, when the Royal family's public opposition to slavery was satirized in a cartoon by James Gillray. He portrayed Queen Charlotte, and their daughters with King George III saying 'O delicious! Delicious!' as he sipped his tea without sugar. In the cartoon, the Queen encourages her daughters to drink the unsweetened tea: "O, my dear Creatures, do but Taste it! You can't think how nice it is without sugar, and then think how much Work you'll save the poor Blackamoors by leaving off the use of it! And above all, remember how much expense it will save your poor Papa! O it's charming cooling Drink." James Gillray was a leading satirist of his time and ridiculed characters across the political spectrum. [101] A review of Gillray's 1792 cartoon shows Charlotte with a broad nose and wide mouth consistent of a woman of African or Moorish heritage. Gillray's caricature showed that he viewed Queen Charlotte as a brown-skinned woman, with Negro, African or Moorish features.

CHAPTER SIX
Abolitionist & Advocate

Wilberforce: Evangelist and Member of Parliament

Another powerful abolitionist ally of King George III and Queen Charlotte was William Wilberforce, a wealthy Evangelical Christian. Wilberforce relentlessly lobbied King George III and the British Parliament, over several decades to abolish slavery and the Parliament repeatedly rejected his appeals.[102] Finally, in 1807, Wilberforce wrote a powerful book titled, _A Letter on the Abolition of the Slave Trade_ that helped to motivate the British Parliament to finally pass the 'Abolition of the Slave Trade Act, in 1808.' The Royal family strongly supported the action of the Parliament to finally end the brutal and inhumane practice and King George III signed the legislation. Note: Wilberforce University in the United States, a Historically Black College in Ohio, is named for William Wilberforce, in recognition of his fight to end slavery. [103]

In 1807, Queen Charlotte joined Wilberforce and others in celebrating passage of the end of slavery in England. Later in 1819, Author W.C. Oulton commented about her reaction to the Abolition of the Slave Trade Act writing, "The abolition of the slave-trade, that nefarious and abominable traffic which had so long been a disgrace to a free country, took place this year, at which the Queen and Princesses expressed great satisfaction."[104] Sadly, although England had abolished slavery on British soil, the vicious international trade of human beings continued throughout the world.

William Wilberforce, Granville Sharp and other abolitionists in America, England and throughout the world had to continue their anti-slavery advocacy for decades and Queen Charlotte continued to support their efforts. While having access and support from the Queen of England did not guarantee them immediate success, they did made progress over several decades in England and in the Colonies. History does not speculate regarding the actual power of Queen Charlotte to have personally ended slavery if she had tried but, her public support for the Abolitionists should be highlighted and remembered.

A LETTER

ON

THE ABOLITION

OF THE

SLAVE TRADE;

ADDRESSED TO THE

FREEHOLDERS AND OTHER INHABITANTS

OF

YORKSHIRE.

BY W. WILBERFORCE, Esq.

" There is neither Greek nor Jew, circumcision nor uncircumcision, Barbarian, Scythian, bond nor free: but CHRIST is all, and in all. Put on therefore bowels of mercies, kindness," &c.—COL. iii. 11. 12.

" GOD hath made of one blood all nations of men, for to dwell on all the face of the earth."—ACTS xvii. 26.

LONDON:

Printed by Luke Hansard & Sons,

FOR T. CADELL AND W. DAVIES, STRAND; And,

J. HATCHARD, PICCADILLY.

1807.

Cover of William Wilberforce's Book to Abolish the Slave Trade, 1807

CHAPTER SIX
Abolitionist & Advocate

British Governor Who Freed Slaves in Colonies

During the American Revolutionary War, King George III appointed the leaders of the British Army who fought the war in the colonies. One of the first appointments he made was John Murray, fourth Earl of Dunmore aka Lord Dunmore, to be the British Governor in Virginia. As Governor, Dunmore led British troops to fight the Revolutionary rebels in Virginia, in the uncharted Appalachian mountain regions, and in the Southern region of the newly formed American colonies. King George III and Queen Charlotte knew Lord Dunmore well since his daughter Lady Augusta Murray (1768-1830) was married to their 6th son, Augustus Frederick. Interestingly, one of the first things Lord Dunmore did when he got to America, was to name a British Military Base in Ohio, after Charlotte, making it the first geographic location in America named for the Queen. The military base was called, "Camp Charlotte" and is the location where a historic treaty was signed agreed between Lord Dunmore and Chief Cornstalk, of the Shawnee tribe.

Plaque at the location of a British-Indian Treaty Signing, at Camp Charlotte, 1774[105]

As the British Army fought the settlers and colonists in the Americas they realized they needed more soldiers to try to put down the rebellion. They were up against American Revolutionary soldiers led by the fierce General George Washington, Thomas Jefferson, Patrick Henry, and other colonial rebels. So, to help recruit new soldiers, Lord Dunmore developed a strategy to secretly encourage enslaved Black people to run away from their plantations and join the British army. First, Dunmore got authority from King George III to offer slaves their freedom if they joined the British Army to fight slave owners. He figured he could get the extra soldiers they needed by offering Black enslaved people their freedom if they ran away, from the plantations. The largest slaveholders in the colonies who were prime targets for his strategy, included George Washington and Thomas Jefferson.[106]

Dunmore turned to British abolitionists like William Wilberforce for help in figuring out how to spread information among the enslaved Africans. Wilberforce, the Abolitionist who worked between the colonies and England, and who was a friend of Queen Charlottes, found a way to secretly pass information among the slaves to inform them they could get their freedom if they ran away. Author Simon Scharma reports that the Blacks enslaved in Virginia, had secret religious meetings where they were told King George III had "hearkened to the gospel and was about to alter the World and set the Negroes Free."[107] Among the enslaved blacks in Virginia and other colonies, King George III took on an exalted status, as a liberator of slaves.

In 1775, Lord Dunmore issued a famous proclamation in the name of King George III that stated, "I do hereby further declare all indented Servants, Negroes or others free that are able and willing to bear Arms, they joining His Majesty's Troops as soon as may be, for the more speedily reducing this Colony to a proper sense of their Duty to His Majesty's Crown and Dignity."[108] Thousands of enslaved blacks heeded this proclamation and joined the British Army and moved to Nova Scotia, Canada. They were called the "Black Patriots."[109] One example of a black patriot was Harry Washington, a man enslaved to George Washington, who escaped to Nova Scotia, Canada and joined the British Army. Perhaps Harry saw Charlotte's picture when it was distributed in Virginia, and believed in Lord Dunmore's offer that King George III was on the side of the slaves.

When they arrived in Nova Scotia, Canada, some of them newly freed people established a free colonies; while others went to England, where they lived free and found low-level paying jobs. Yet, others returned to Africa to establish colonies in Sierra Leone and Liberia. It is not known if King George III and Queen Charlotte met any of the enslaved Blacks when they managed to get to England but, it is a matter of history that the Royal couple's efforts resulted in thousands of people in the colonies, achieving their freedom.

Abolitionist & Advocate

By His Excellency the Right Honorable JOHN Earl of DUNMORE, His Majesty's Lieutenant and Governor General of the Colony and Dominion of Virginia, and Vice Admiral of the same.

A PROCLAMATION.

AS I have ever entertained Hopes, that an Accommodation might have taken Place between GREAT-BRITAIN and this Colony, without being compelled by my Duty to this most disagreeable but now absolutely neceffary Step, rendered fo by a Body of armed Men unlawfully affembled, firing on His MAJESTY's Tenders, and the formation of an Army, and that Army now on their March to attack His Majesty's Troops and deftroy the well difpofed Subjects of this Colony. To defeat fuch reafonable Purpofes, and that all fuch Traitors, and their Abettors, may be brought to Juftice, and that the Peace, and good Order of this Colony may be again reftored, which the ordinary Courfe of the Civil Law is unable to effect; I have thought fit to iffue this my Proclamation, hereby declaring, that until the aforefaid good Purpofes can be obtained, I do in Virtue of the Power and Authority to ME given, by His Majefty, determine to execute Martial Law, and caufe the fame to be executed throughout this Colony; and to the end that Peace and good Order may the fooner be reftored, I do require every Perfon capable of bearing Arms, to refort to His MAJESTY's STANDARD, or be looked upon as Traitors to His MAJESTY's Crown and Government, and thereby become liable to the Penalty the Law inflicts upon fuch Offences; fuch as forfeiture of Life, confifcation of Lands, &c. &c. And I do hereby further declare all indented Servants, Negroes, or others, (appertaining to Rebels,) free that are able and willing to bear Arms, they joining His MAJESTY's Troops as foon as may be, for the more fpeedily reducing this Colony to a proper Senfe of their Duty, to His MAJESTY's Crown and Dignity. I do further order, and require, all His MAJESTY's Leige Subjects, to retain their Quitrents, or any other Taxes due or that may become due, in their own Cuftody, till fuch Time as Peace may be again reftored to this at prefent moft unhappy Country, or demanded of them for their former falutary Purpofes, by Officers properly authorifed to receive the fame.

GIVEN under my Hand on board the Ship WILLIAM, off Norfolk, the 7th Day of November, in the sixteenth Year of His Majefty's Reign.

DUNMORE.

(GOD fave the KING.)

Lord Dunmore's 1775 "Emancipation Proclamation" freeing blacks to join British Army. [110]

CHAPTER SIX
Abolitionist & Advocate

Olaudah Equiano: Former Slave and Abolitionist

One of the most remarkable people who wrote a letter to Queen Charlotte to advocate against the Trans-Atlantic slave trade, was a smart young man from the Igbo tribe, on the west coast of Africa, named Olaudah Equiano. Olaudah was sold into captivity at the age of 11 and grew up hoping to be freed by his British master but, instead he was betrayed and sold into further slavery. His new purchaser was Robert King, a Quaker merchant who conducted trade in sugar and slaves between the West Indies and the American South. Recognizing Olaudah's talents, King promoted him to increasingly responsible positions in the human trade business and allowed him to purchase his freedom on July 10, 1766. Olaudah was very religious and studied Christianity and thirty years later, in 1779, he sought ordination by the Bishop of London, to be a missionary to West Africa but, was rejected. He then became a leader in the fight to abolish slavery and traveled widely giving first-person accounts describing the evils of slavery. By 1788, his leadership gained momentum and tens of thousands of signatures poured into the British Parliament demanding the abolishment of slavery.[111]

Olaudah Equiano

Olaudah Equiano

On March 21, 1788, the year before he published a best-selling book, Equiano delivered a slave trade petition to Queen Charlotte calling for the British Parliament to outlaw slavery. His petition strengthened the Queen's opposition to slavery and helped persuade the Parliament to ultimately pass laws to outlaw slavery, although it took them another twenty years to do it.

The following year, in 1789, Equiano wrote a book called, *The Interesting Narrative of the Life of Olaudah Equiano, or Gustavus Vassa, the African, Written by Himself.* The book gained a strong following in England among the Abolitionist community, including Granville Sharpe and gained strong support from John Wesley, the founder of Methodism, who had migrated to Savannah, Georgia, at the invitation of Georgia founder James Oglethorpe. John Wesley called Equiano's book, "more use to our cause than half the people in the country." [112] While it is not known if Queen Charlotte read Equiano's book, it is likely she did because it was a best seller and she was an avid reader.

Appeal from Antoine Benezet

Another abolitionist who appealed to King George III and Queen Charlotte to stop slavery, was Antoine Bénézet, (1713-1784). Benezet was a Frenchman and Quaker who fled from France with his family, lived in England for a period of years and later moved to Germantown, an area of Philadelphia, Pennsylvania. After settling in Germantown, he married a daughter in the wealthy Marriott family and gained considerable financial resources. [113] Benezet was an educator who came to the belief that black people were not inferior and were intelligent people who could be productive and meaningful contributors to society. To further his beliefs about education, he offered evening classes to black people, mostly in his own home. Benezet's vision and abolitionist leadership were demonstrated when he founded the Society for the Relief of Free Negroes Unlawfully Held in Bondage. After his death, Benjamin Franklin and Dr. Benjamin Rush renamed the organization as the Pennsylvania Society for Promoting the Abolition of Slavery. Benezet also established the first public school for girls in North America; and in 1770, he convinced his fellow Quakers to build the first free day school in America, called the Negro School, which operated into the nineteenth century. He promoted abolitionism in Pennsylvania a hundred years before slavery was abolished in America.

On August 25, 1783, Benezet wrote a letter to Queen Charlotte asking her to consider the plight of those enslaved in America, and the West Indies. He warned her of a curse he believed could occur to a nation that promoted such injustice. [114] Benezet believed the practice of slavery was inconsistent with Christianity and common justice, and he was appalled that religious leaders in America, supported slavery. It is not known if Queen Charlotte answered his letter or met with him but, given her known support for the abolitionist philosophy and her friendship with Quakers, she very likely read Benezet's articles, letters and epistles, where he sought to eradicate slave ownership among the Quaker people in America and England.

Abolitionist & Advocate

Portrait of Queen Charlotte, by Alan Ramsey[115]

Queen Charlotte's Portrait, Used in Colonies with Enslaved People

As noted earlier, Lord Dunmore urged enslaved Blacks to run-away and join the British Army. To strengthen the claim that King George was on the side of the enslaved blacks, Lord Dunmore passed the word among the enslaved populations that Queen Charlotte, was a mixed race woman, with black heritage. This claim was supported by copies of portraits of Charlotte, that served as proof to the slaves, that King George III accepted black people. The portrait artists who painted Queen Charlotte's picture showed her thick hair and light brown skin tone and mixed-race features, recognized by blacks in the Americas.

One of the artists who painted Charlotte portraits was Alan Ramsey, (1713-1784) a Scottish painter who lived in England, and who served many years as the official court artist. Ramsey painted the official Coronation portraits of George III and Queen Charlotte, and showed several poses of the Queen in official Coronation gowns, with different hairstyles. Over the years, Ramsey came to know the Royal couple very well, and they trusted him.[116] In his paintings, one can see Charlotte portrayed the Queen as a lovely mulatto woman, with thick curly hair and broad features. During his career, his art had a global impact—even in the colonies. Today, his 233 paintings of King George III, Queen Charlotte, and other famous figures can be found at the National Portrait Gallery, London; The Derby Museum and Art Gallery, in the United Kingdom, the Glasgow Museum, Scotland, and many other galleries around the world.

CHAPTER SIX
Abolitionist & Advocate

Alan Ramsey, Self Portrait circa 1737-39 [117]

Alan Ramsey's family was unique since it included people of diverse racial backgrounds and members with racially conscious attitudes. Ramsey's wife Margaret Lindsey was the niece of William Murray, 1st Earl of Mansfield, Chief Justice of England, who made the 1772 Somersett landmark court decision that ended slavery in the British Empire. Lord Mansfield had raised a mulatto girl in his household named Dido Elizabeth Lindsay, whose story is featured in the 2014 film "Belle," produced by Fox Searchlight Pictures. [118] Dido was born to an enslaved mother and white British mariner in the British Islands and after her mother's death, her father took her to live with his Uncle Chief Justice Lord Mansfield. Since Charlotte was the Queen during this same time-period and Alan Ramsey was her artist, perhaps she and Dido interacted and recognized their similar mixed race backgrounds.

According to Mario de Valdes y Cocom, it was copies of Alan Ramsey's paintings of Queen Charlotte that were used by the Abolitionists as *de facto* support for the cause of freeing slaves. [119] As the official Court artist, it is unlikely that Ramsey would have provided pictures of Queen Charlotte to Lord Dunmore for him to disseminate in the colonies, unless the King and Queen approved. Their approval was another indication of their support for the efforts of the abolitionist movement, to build up the British army with black soldiers. As noted earlier, Harry Washington, a man enslaved by General George Washington, was one of the Black men who ran away from Washington's plantation, to join the British army as a Black Loyalist. Perhaps Harry Washington saw a copy of the portrait of Queen Charlotte and was persuaded by the portrait. [120]

On March 25, 1807, when the Act for the Abolition of the Slave Trade was passed and in 1808 when it became law, Queen Charlotte provided an official reaction making it clear to the Parliament and the British people, that she and King George III supported ending the brutal practice of slavery in the United Kingdom. When the slave trade was abolished in the British Empire and British traders were discouraged from the Atlantic slave trade, it encouraged the British to press other European states to abolish their slave trades.

CHAPTER SIX
Abolitionist & Advocate

Nova Scotia, Queens County, Canada—Destination for Black Loyalists

More evidence to indicate the people in Canada believed Queen Charlotte supported the Abolitionist movement was the naming of Queens County, Canada, after her. This area of Canada is where Nova Scotia is located, and was settled by approximately 3,000 African Americans who supported the British, during the American Revolution. When Lord Dunmore, offered enslaved Black people their freedom and assisted them to repatriate to British Canada, the area was named Novia Scotia, Queens County, Canada. The Black Loyalists who ran away from the plantations during the American Revolutionary War, and fought on behalf of Great Britain believed they were fighting not only for their own freedom, but for the ultimate abolition of slavery in North America.

CHAPTER SEVEN
15 Children in 21 Years

During the first 21 years of their marriage, Queen Charlotte gave birth to 15 children--nine sons and six daughters. Sadly, two of the boys did not live past infancy. Infant death was not unusual in the 1700's since health and medical care was limited. However, 13 of the children in the Royal family did reach adulthood and were able to live full lives. During the 1700's, it was impressive for any woman to give birth to 15 children, and to raise most of them. Charlotte was an excellent mother who raised each child with their own unique personality, skills and talents. Although the Queen had servants, governesses, and medical attendants, she personally participated in their child rearing and did not completely "hand off" her children to others, as was often done in Royal families.

Johan Zoffany's Portrait of King George III, Queen Charlotte, and six oldest children

George and Charlotte taught their children a variety of subjects at home, with the assistance of tutors. Their learning approach was like a modern day homeschool environment with lots of resources. One of Queen Charlotte's primary teaching assistants was Lady Charlotte Finch (February 1725-July 1813). Lady Finch served as Royal governess to the children for over thirty years and they were all taught reading, astronomy, botany, and science. And, like Charlotte was taught as a child, the

CHAPTER SEVEN
15 Children in 21 Years

Royal children learned how to play music in a family ensemble. When the boys came of age, they went off to military school and college, while the girls stayed home and learned art, music and decorating. As young adults, the boys got accustomed to extravagant princely lifestyles, scandalous romances, and adventuresome military careers.

In some cases their sons became rebellious and started to resist the authority of their parents. One example of a rebellious son was George Augustus Frederick, Prince of Wales. George Augusus actually fought his parents over the power of the throne—a situation caused when King George III had difficulty serving due to his illness and periodic mental crisises. While several of the sons became problems, the daughters stayed close to home and their mother. Several of the daughters did not marry and lived the lives of spinsters.

Queen Charlotte with two of her daughters. Painting by Alan Ramsey, 1769

15 Children in 21 Years

Small Pox Vaccinations

Queen Charlotte's intelligence and analytic skills were shown in her willingness to embrace innovative child-rearing practices. For example, she had a keen understanding of the concept of medical prevention, and how vaccinations could protect her children from disease. In the late 1700's, she became a pioneer in the use of inoculations against smallpox—a terrible disease that had killed millions of people for centuries. Charlotte allowed her children to be vaccinated during the early discovery period of the medical tool. When they inoculated their children, it was consider by many to be a risky decision but, since King George III and Queen Charlotte had studied science they took the risk.

Portrait of Charlotte with one of her children, by artist Frances Cotes, 1767. Lady Mary Coke called the likeness "so like that it could not be mistaken for any other person"[121]

Charlotte learned about the small pox vaccines during the mid-1700's, when a young scientist named Dr. Edward Jenner of Gloucestershire, England, introduced her to his vaccine research. Like Queen Charlotte, Jenner had been raised in a country environment and had a strong interest in science and nature. At the age of 13, he became fascinated with stories he heard from dairy maids who believed smallpox could be cured by rubbing something called "cowpox" from cattle on the skins of human beings and Jenner never forgot the stories and folklore. When he grew up, Jenner experimented with cowpox and discovered the smallpox vaccine.

Later, when he became a doctor at St. George's Hospital, in London, Jenner was elected a fellow of the Royal Society, an organization that included the most brilliant scientists, botanists, philosophers and artists of the time. Jenner continued his research on the smallpox vaccine and made great strides, although his work was controversial.[122] However, despite the controversy, King George III, and Queen Charlotte believed in his experimental procedures and in 1782, they had their children vaccinated. Sadly, two of their sons—Prince Albert and Prince Octavius died from the side effects of the smallpox vaccination. Lady Charlotte Finch, the children's governess, reported that Queen Charlotte "cried vastly at first and…though very reasonable – she dwelt on her good fortune in having thirteen healthy children…and she was very much hurt by her loss and the King also."[123]

The Legacies of King George III and Queen Charlotte

George III and Charlotte's children had varied personalities and talents. Some of them became famous leaders of England including King George IV; King William IV; King Ernest Augustus I; and King George V. One of their granddaughters--Queen Victoria, was one of the most popular descendants of the Royal family. The modern Royal family in 21st century England headed by Queen Elizabeth and her children are also among their descendants. One indication of the family lineage that connected them with their ancestors King George III and Queen Charlotte was on July 22, 2013, when Prince William and his wife Kate Middleton named their first child George, and in 2015, when they named their second child Charlotte.

Brief Bios of the Royal Children of King George III and Queen Charlotte

Listed below are brief descriptions and highlights about the children of Queen Charlotte and King George III:

- **George Augustus Frederick, Prince of Wales,** (1762-1830) was the oldest son of King George III and Queen Charlotte. When King George III first developed periodic bouts with mental illness, George IV petitioned the British Parliament to appoint him Prince Regent, so he could be the King, instead of his father. The Parliament refused his request for decades until King George IIII became elderly, and his mental illness became worse. Finally, on February 6, 1811 the Prince of Wales succeeded at becoming Prince Regent under the terms of the

15 Children in 21 Years

Regency Act. When his father died, he ascended to the British throne after serving nine years as Regent. He lived extravagantly, did not get along very well with his Mother Queen Charlotte. [124]

- **Prince Frederick Duke of York** (1763-1827) was the second eldest child and second son of George III and Queen Charlotte. He became heir presumptive to the British throne on the death of his father in 1820 but, never became King because he died before his older brother, George IV. [125]

Son William Henry was targeted by George Washington for kidnapping during the American Revolutionary War [126]

- **William Henry, Duke of Clarence** (1765-1837) was the third son of George III and Charlotte. Based on his age, he was not expected to become king. He joined the Royal Navy when he was 13 and fought in New York during the American War of Independence. While in America, George Washington approved a plot to kidnap William but, the plot did not come to fruition because the British heard of it and assigned guards to him. Duke William had up until then walked around New York unescorted. [127] At the age of 64 years old, William Henry became king when his brother George IV died, in 1830. He reigned as King William IV of Great Britain and Hanover (1765-1837). [128]

- **Charlotte Augusta Matilda,** (1766-1828) was the eldest daughter of King George III and Queen Charlotte. She was called "Princess Royal" since she was named Charlotte after her mother. Like her mother, Princess Royal excelled in artistry and botany. She was artistic and designed beautiful porcelain vases. [129] Note: Princess Royal's portrait photo below shows thick, kinky hair that she inherited from her mother, revealing their Moorish and mixed-race ancestry.

- **Edward Augustus, Duke of Kent** (1767-1820) was known as Prince Edward, Duke of Kent and Strathearn. He was the fourth son of George III and Queen Charlotte and he supported charitable works, such as the Literary Fund and introduced regimental schools for children. He was interested in social experiments and supported anti-slavery and abolitionist causes. Prince Edward was the father of Queen Victoria, Charlotte's granddaughter, a popular Queen of England. [130]

Charlotte Augusta Matilda, Princess Royal[131]

- **Augusta Sophia** (1768-1840) was the second daughter of King George III and Queen Charlotte. She was home schooled by Charlotte and a staff of governesses and tutors. She was a good student and enjoyed learning modern languages, history, geography, music, art and needlework. Augusta was energetic and played cricket and football with her brothers. She never married. [132]

- **Elizabeth** (1770-1840) was the third daughter of King George III and Queen Charlotte. She was homeschooled by her mother and Queen Charlotte approved every book Elizabeth read. Elizabeth was taught English, modern foreign languages, geography, history, music, art. She had excellent taste in music and art is credited with designing a trellis on the ceiling of her mother's bedroom at Frogmore. In 1795, Elizabeth created the popular icon "Cupid," which has existed for centuries as a love symbol. She published Cupid in a series of prints titled, "The Birth and

Triumph," under the name Lady Dashwood. At the age of 47, she married Prince Frederick of Hesse-Homburg.[133]

- **Ernest Augustus, Duke of Cumberland,** (1771-1851) reigned as King Ernest of Hanover. He was the fifth son of George III and Queen Charlotte. He was inducted into the secret order of the Knights of the Garter, a fraternity among aristocrats. He attended the University of Göttingen, in Germany, a school established by his Great-Grandfather George II. Ernest was a rebel and often fought against his parent's wishes. For example, in 1815, Ernest married his cousin, Charlotte's niece Princess Frederica, from Mecklenburg, Germany. Charlotte did not like Frederica because she had been married twice before, and was twice widowed. Charlotte refused to receive Frederica as her daughter-in-law and this created a family scandal and bad relationships.[134]

- **Augustus Frederick, Duke of Sussex** (1773-1843) was the sixth son of George III and Charlotte. He was a sickly child and when he became a young man, he was unable to join the army due to his ill health caused by asthma. He attended University of Göttingen, in Germany and in 1832, Augustus almost went blind but, an experimental cataract operation saved his sight. He was over 6'3" tall and was gifted musically with a three-octave range, enabling him to sing in the family ensemble. Augustus Frederick was a strong abolitionist.[135]

- **Adolphus Frederick, Duke of Cambridge** (1774-1850) was the seventh son of George III and Queen Charlotte. On June 2, 1786, he was made a Knight of the Garter, in the Royal fraternity. Like his brothers, he went to the University of Göttingen, in Germany where he studied the classics, theology, and fencing. In 1790, Adolphus became a colonel in the Hanoverian army where he fought against Napoleon. He returned to England where he was made Military Commander of the Home District and Colonel-in-Chief of the Coldstream Guards. On November 26, 1813, he was promoted to Field Marshal in the British army.[136]

15 Children in 21 Years

- **Princess Mary** (1776-1857) was the 4th daughter of King George III and Queen Charlotte. She was born at Buckingham House and was home-schooled by her mother, governesses and teachers under the direction of Lady Charlotte Finch. Mary learned English, French, German, geography, history, music, art and needlework. She was musically talented, became skilled at drawing in chalk and enjoyed live theater.[137] Princess Mary married her cousin, Prince William Frederick, Duke of Gloucester, and lived near her parents in Windsor and London. She had no children.

- **Sophia** (1777-1848) was the fifth daughter of George III and Queen Charlotte. She was born at Windsor Castle and was home-schooled by Charlotte and Lady Charlotte Finch, with the assistance of governesses and tutors. Sophia learned English, French, German, geography, history, music, art and needlework. She never married and it was rumored that she may have had an out-of-wedlock child.

- **Octavius** (1779-1783) was the thirteenth child and eighth son of George III and Queen Charlotte and he was the favorite son of King George. When Octavius he was four years old he was inoculated against smallpox and he became sick and died from the side-effects. His death was a terrible tragedy for King George who reportedly said, "There will be no heaven for me if Octavius is not there."[138] King George never recovered from the loss of his baby boy.

- **Prince Alfred** (1780-1782) was the ninth and youngest son of George III and Queen Charlotte. He was christened in the great council chamber at St James' Palace by the Archbishop of Canterbury. His wet nurse was the wife of an East India captain. Alfred's health was so poor that he was sent with Lady Charlotte Finch and a physician, to make use of healing salt waters at a remote location. However, he wasn't cured and died at the age of two.

CHAPTER SEVEN
15 Children in 21 Years

- **Princess Amelia** (1783-1810) was the fifteenth child and sixth daughter of King George III and Queen Charlotte. Her father enjoyed sitting on the carpet and playing games with her. Amelia grew to be a tall and slender woman who was graceful in demeanor. Like her sisters, her education was supervised by Lady Charlotte Finch and she was taught English, French, geography, music, art and needlework. She played the piano well and was skilled at horseback riding. Unfortunately, when Amelia was 15 she became ill with tuberculosis and by 18 years old she developed a painful bacterial skin infection. She died young at the age of 27.[139]

CHAPTER EIGHT
Books, Art and Astronomy

From all accounts, during their 60 year marriage King George III and Queen Charlotte were faithful to each other. Faithfulness in marriage was a unique quality among Royalty in Europe, and George III and Charlotte deserve praise for their loyalty. They shared an enthusiastic love of learning in many areas including supporting global explorers, art, science, astronomy, music and botany and farming. The King sponsored explorers like Captain John Cook, a British Naval Captain, navigator and explorer who, in 1770, discovered and charted New Zealand, and the Great Barrier Reef of Australia, on his ship HMB Endeavour.[140] Note: the fifth NASA Space Shuttle "Endeavour" was named after Captain Cook's ship "HMB Endeavor" that in 1768, sailed into the South Pacific and around Tahiti. During that voyage Captain Cook and his crew observed the passage of Venus between the earth and the sun.[141] One of the waterways in New Zealand explored by Captain Cook was later named Queen Charlotte Sound, in honor of Charlotte.

Portrait of Charlotte by Joshua Reynolds

Even though the King and Queen could have been lofty, aloof and arrogant, they were respectful of the knowledge of others. As lifelong learners, the Royal Couple worked with philosophers, scientists, artists, scholars in medicine, religion, politics, music, the arts and social justice intellectuals who advocated the abolition of slavery. Through their collaborations, the Royal Couple established several institutions and centers of learning and supported cutting edge research. One institution King George III established in 1768, was the Royal Academy of Arts, an institution that exists today, and is

Books, Art and Astronomy

known for its exhibitions of paintings of Queen Charlotte, and many other portraits of people, who lived during their era.

While King George III and Queen Charlotte were popular in England, King George III was intensely disliked in the American Colonies. The colonists hated being taxed by the British and it was under George III's authority that the despised Stamp Act was instituted in 1764. The Stamp Act made the Colonists pay heavy taxes and they felt it was unfair. George Grenville, the British Prime Minister at the time, convinced the British Parliament and King George III that the Stamp Act would raise money for Britain, in the American Colonies.[142] Colonists including George Washington, Thomas Jefferson and other Founding Fathers opposed the Stamp Act taxation and their opposition led to mistrust of King George III and caused a lot of unrest, in the colonies.

In 1773, when Lord North, a new Prime Minister of the Parliament took over from George Grenville, the Parliament then passed a new tax on tea in the American colonies. This extra tax angered the colonists even more as they complained about being taxed without representation. The tea tax led to the famous rebellion when Samuel Adams and the Knights of Liberty dumped crates of tea in the Boston Harbor Bay. This rebellious event known as the "Boston Tea Party" increased the confrontation between King George III, and the colonies and the conflict eventually led to the American Revolutionary War. While Queen Charlotte wasn't directly involved in the colonial issues and the pending war, she was aware of it and witnessed the pressures on her husband. The intensity of the pending Revolutionary War was made even more difficult because King George III experienced bouts of hysteria, nervousness, and stress from the Porphyria disease he had contracted, that caused periodic illness, behavior difficulties and mental illness.

Book Collectors

King George III was the most passionate book collector in the history of the Monarchy. In 1823, his extensive library was given to the British Museum. The collection contains books printed mainly in Britain, Europe, and North America from the mid-15th to the early 19th centuries. There are 65,000 volumes of printed books and 19,000 pamphlets, including a copy of the Gutenberg Bible. Many of the books reflect King George III's interests in agriculture and architecture and are annotated in his hand. His library also includes letters and books that reveal him as a family man. As the writer, Thomas de Quincy (1785-

1859) noted, "His care extended even to the dressing of the books in appropriate bindings, and...to their health. The displays include a selection of the King's bookbinding tools..."[143]

Queen's Library at Frogmore House, painting by Charlies Wild[144]

     The King's library revealed his domestic life with the Queen and their children. Included in the library are lists of gifts they exchanged, specially commissioned tableware for tea and coffee drinking, writing sets and gaming pieces. The exhibit shows how music was central to their lives and how the Royal Couple played a variety of instruments and had a private music ensemble with their children. Some of the featured instruments include a stringed instrument called a claviorgan, harpsichord, and the King's personal flute.

     Queen Charlotte was also a great collector of books. She built an elaborate personal library at their home at Frogmore, that included botanical books that she used to teach their children. The Queen's staff stacked her books in the plentiful rooms, where she read them at her leisure. Her collection of books is on display at the British Museum and Royal Collection Trust.

CHAPTER EIGHT
Books, Art and Astronomy

Art

King George III and Queen Charlotte were enthusiastic patrons of art and artists. They became were friends with their official court artists and sat for numerous portraits. Some of the artists who painted them were leading British artists of the 18th century, including Allan Ramsay, Thomas Gainsborough, Joshua Reynolds and Johan Zoffany. These artists painted individual portraits and recorded scenes of the Royal family and their children. The Royal couple paid special attention to supporting artists and acquiring special collections. Joshua Reynolds, who had painted a number portraits of Queen Charlotte was a leading English portraitist of the 18th century and served as the first President of the Royal Academy, established by King George, in 1768.[145]

Portrait of Charlotte by artist Benjamin West, hanging at Yale University.[146]

During the time of the disputes with the American colonies, George III commissioned a series of paintings from the American artist Benjamin West, who did portraits of soldiers fighting in the Revolutionary War. West was a friend of Benjamin Franklin, a founding father of the United States. West moved from Pennsylvania to London where he struck up a friendship with artist Joshua Reynolds, and was invited to paint several individual portraits of Charlotte. One of the portraits he painted shows her in a purple gown, and hangs at Yale University. Her thick, textured, hair is styled on top of her head. Another portrait by West painted in 1799, hangs in the East Wing, at Buckingham Palace, and also features the Queen's thick textured hair.

Books, Art and Astronomy

Kings Observatory aka Kew Observatory, established in 1769, by King George III[147]

Astronomy

When his health was good, King George III was very active in a variety of things. As a young man, he studied science and astronomy and loved viewing the stars. He established the King's Astronomical Observatory in 1769, on the Richmond Estate, near the Kew Gardens where he and Queen Charlotte spent hours teaching their children astronomy. The Royal couple's absorption in astronomy influenced and helped inspire astronomical observatories all over the world including—the Armagh Observatory and Dunsink Observatory, that are located in Ireland.[148]

King George III enjoyed collecting scientific instruments that are currently on display at the Science Museum, on Exhibition Road, in South Kensington, London. The King's instrument collection is one of the largest collections of scientific apparatus developed in the 18th century. In 1761, he commissioned instruments from George Adams of Fleet Street, an instrument maker who made George III a silver microscope.[149] The microscope Adams created was ornate with figurines and objective lenses used to examine objects. The microscope is just one example of the collection of instrumentation owned by George III. The King also commissioned sophisticated clocks, barometers, and watches and was fascinated with understanding their mechanisms.

Books, Art and Astronomy

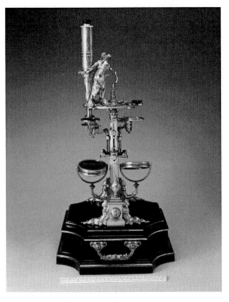

Microscope made by instrument maker George Adams, for King George III[150]

First Lady's Comet

The Royal family spent many nights viewing the stars, with their children at Windsor Palace. Joining them for the viewings were William and Caroline Herschel, a famous brother and sister astronomer team, who lived near Windsor Palace. William Herschel (1738-1822) was a well-known musician as well as a brilliant astronomer who discovered new planets in the solar system. His sister Caroline Lucretia Herschel, (1750-1848) was a musician and also assisted her brother with his astronomy work.[151] The Herschel's were from Hanover, Germany, a region Charlotte knew well, since it was near her home in Mecklenburg.

Caroline Hershel, astronomer who named comet for Queen Charlotte [152]

Caroline and William were quite ambitious with their careers. In 1780, they left Hanover, Germany to move to Bath, England to advance their study of astronomy.[153] Caroline helped her brother by grinding and polishing mirrors for his telescopes and copying his records. She also was also fascinated with the stars. One evening om 1781, while conducting his research of the stars, William discovered the planet Uranus. He gave credit to his sister Caroline for helping him to make this incredible scientific discovery. When his discovery of Uranus became known, King George III rewarded him with an appointment, as the official court astronomer. [154] Hershel wanted to name Uranus "Georgin Sidus" after the King but, another astronomer suggested the name Uranus, after the ancient Greek deity Ouranos, and that name was selected. [155] The King also gave William Hershel the title "Sir William Hershel."

Queen Charlotte had great admiration for Caroline Hershel's astronomy skills and encouraged her to become an astronomer in her own right. The Queen knew that Caroline was good at astronomy and that in addition to assisting her brother, the Queen encouraged Caroline to make her own discoveries. William gave his sister a telescope so, Caroline could view the stars on her own. Diarist Fanny Burney wrote that one evening when she was visiting Windsor Palace, William came to share the news with His Majesty and the Royal Family, that Caroline had discovered a new comet. Fanny wrote, "…while I was playing piquet with Mrs. Schwellenberg, the Princess Augusta came into the room, and asked her if she chose to go into the garden and look at it (the comet). She declined the offer, and the princess then made it to me. I was glad to accept it, for all sorts of reasons. We found him (William Herschel) at his telescope, and I mounted some steps to look through it. The comet was very small, and had nothing grand or striking in its appearance, but it is the First Lady's comet, and I was very desirous to see it." [156] Caroline named her first discovery the "First Lady's Comet," in honor of the Queen Charlotte's encouragement and support of her work.

40 Foot Telescope constructed by William and Caroline Herschel

When King George III heard that Caroline had discovered eight comets through her own astronomical skills, he gave her brother William an added stipend of 50 pounds annually, to be paid to her. The King had to give the money to William since women were not allowed to be not paid by the government for their own scientific work. However, being paid—even though it was through her brother, made Caroline

Herschel the first woman in England's history to have a paid government appointment.[157]

In 1787, Sir Joseph Banks, President of the Royal Society, Director of the Kew Gardens and the explorer that King George III and Queen Charlotte endorsed, humorously suggested Caroline's Royal pension should come from Queen Charlotte rather than George III, since Caroline was "The First Lady's Comet Hunter." Banks was aware of the Queen's encouragement of Caroline's astronomical career and was giving her a compliment. In 1828, Caroline Herschel was awarded a gold medal from the Royal Astronomical Society. [158]

CHAPTER NINE
Queen of Botany

The Queen made the Kew Botanical Gardens her special project and under her stewardship in the late 1700's and early 1800's, the Kew gardens became one of the most famous botanical gardens in the world. Charlotte and King George III enjoyed botany and growing flowers and plants and spent many hours in their gardens. The King focused on innovative agricultural ideas and developments and became known in friendly cartoons and satires with the nickname, "Farmer George."[159] The Queen's love of botany was so well known by the British people that they fondly gave her the honorary title of "Queen of Botany."[160] In her later years, Charlotte used her knowledge of botany to lay out a new garden at the Frogmore estate, with rare and unusual trees and plants.

Charlotte by Monogamist JR, Watercolor, dated 1762[161]

In 1791, when King George III bought Charlotte the Queen's Cottage, at Kew Gardens she grew lilacs, primroses and other wallflowers. [162] She called the herbarium at Frogmore, "her little paradise." It had a greenhouse with herbs and a flower garden that included spirea, honeysuckle, birches, Spanish chestnuts and laburnum trees. Charlotte installed new features in the herbarium including a thatched hermitage, a barn and a Gothic ruin designed by her daughter, Princess Elizabeth. [163] Charlotte taught her daughters about how to dry foreign and native plants and other botany skills.

Queen of Botany

In the 21st century, collections of living and stored materials at the Kew Botanical Gardens are still used by scholars from various countries. The herbarium houses over seven million specimens and plays a significant role in research about plant biodiversity on Earth. The collections of preserved specimens that document the identity of plants serve as a reference of plant identification, research and education and plant biodiversity.[164] Some of the raw plant materials and artifacts date back to Queen Charlotte's involvement hundreds of years ago. In addition to the specimens collected by historically important plant collectors and explorers, the collection includes botany books, pamphlets, maps, plans and pictures.

Flower Named for Queen Charlotte

Joseph Banks, the renowned British explorer (1743 – 1820) was one of Charlotte's mentors in botany. For years, Banks traveled the world with Captain Cook, on the ship "Endeavor" and they explored South America, Tahiti, New Zealand and Australia. As one of the most famous explorers of his day, Banks made many discoveries and collected samples of fish, animals, and plants. After Banks completed a series of worldwide explorations, King George III appointed him to be director of the Kew Gardens.

Bird of Paradise plant, originally named by Joseph Banks, in honor of Queen Charlotte

Queen of Botany

Director of Kew Gardens, Botanist Joseph Banks, painted by Joshua Reynolds, 1773

As director of the Kew Gardens, Banks shared his knowledge of botany with the King and Queen. Together, they sent botanists around the world to collect plants from different countries and Banks examined the plants, their properties and possible food and medicinal applications. Banks was a highly-regarded philosopher and leader who for 41 years, was president of the exclusive Royal Society, the oldest scientific organization in Great Britain. Note: one of the earlier presidents of the Royal Society was Sir Isaac Newton. [165]

Charlotte's ability to keep pace with intellectuals like Banks, and other scholars indicates her intelligence and grasp of sophisticated knowledge. In 1773, Banks named a beautiful, exotic plant from Cape of Good Hope, in South Africa, 'Strelitzia Reginae' in honor of Queen Charlotte. "Strelitzia" referred to Charlotte's hometown of Mecklenburg-Strelitz and 'Reginae' means, "of the Queen." [166] Over the years, the plant's name changed to Bird of Paradise. It is interesting that Banks selected a flower from Africa to name after Queen Charlotte. One might speculate as to whether he saw mixed race African people in South Africa, who looked like Charlotte and named the plant in honor of her Moorish/African heritage.

In 1813, when the Queen was getting older, she and two of her daughters visited Joseph Banks and his wife at their home at Spring Grove, England. In memory of their long-lasting relationship, Queen Charlotte gave Banks and his family a Silver Kettle and Spirit Lamp. Those items are on display today at the National Library of Australia. [167]

CHAPTER NINE
Queen of Botany

Remodeling Frogmore

When Charlotte transformed Frogmore Gardens into a botanical garden, and she selected key experts to assist her with developing the gardens. Her friend Lady Holderness recommended a Reverend Christopher Alderson, (1737-1814) who was a landscape gardener and poet. When the Queen interviewed him she learned that Rev. Alderson was born in Westmoreland, England and had achieved prominence as a garden designer. She was impressed with him and invited him to start working for her on February 7, 1791. Alderson was described by one of Charlotte's daughters as having "infinite taste in laying out places."

Rev. Alderson helped Charlotte transform the plain unimaginative and flat gardens surrounding Frogmore into a beautiful landscape filled with glades, walks, man-made lakes, and wooded mounds. [168] According to biographer Hedley, Queen Charlotte knew how she wanted the garden to look and told her son, Prince Augustus, "My chief plants are to be natives of England and all such foreign ones as will thrive in our soil."[169] Queen Charlotte spared no expense on her gardens in 1791, spent about £1000 a year at Frogmore.[170] Note: in 1791 1,000 British pounds were roughly equivalent to $145,000, in 2015 U.S. dollars. (Calculated at www.measuringworth.com).

The Herbarium

Another botanical expert referred by Duchess Portland to Queen Charlotte, was Rev. John Lightfoot (1735-1788) who served as chaplain and botanical advisor to the Duchess. One evening, Lady-in-Waiting Fanny Burney invited Rev. Lightfoot to dine with the Queen and her daughters and he told them about his herbarium. He shared a book he had written titled, "Flora Scotica" which pioneered the scientific study of plants and fungi of Scotland. The Queen and her daughters were fascinated with his book. [171] In recognition of his outstanding scientific work, Sir Joseph Banks invited Rev. Lightfoot to become a Fellow of the Royal Society.

Queen of Botany

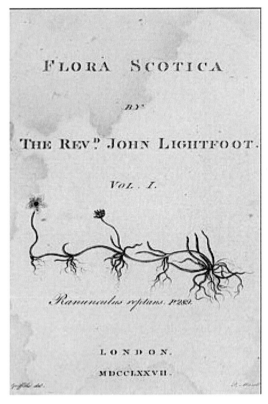

Herbal book titled *Flora Scotica*, written in 1777, by Reverend John Lightfoot

Unfortunately, Rev. Lightfoot died suddenly—a distressing loss to the Queen, Duchess Portland and the girls, who celebrated his work. Joseph Banks wrote to a friend "...the melancholy news of our esteemed friend Mr. Lightfoot has no doubt come to your ears long before now. His botanic collections which were quite respectable have been purchased by the Queen as her majesty has lately applied herself considerably to the study of botany. They will have I hope, due honor done to them." [172] The Queen purchased Rev. Lightfoot's herbarium for 100 guineas and relocated it to Frogmore, so her daughters Princess Augusta and Princess Elizabeth could continue their study botany at his herbarium. Today, most of the Lightfoot herbarium still exists at the Herbarium of the Royal Botanical Gardens, Kew. [173] These are the same Kew Gardens when Prince Charles became Patron, in July 2016.

Botany Book Dedicated to Charlotte

One of Charlotte's most influential mentors was The Right Honorable John Stuart, 3rd Earl of Bute (1713-1792). Earl Bute was the trusted member of the Court who advised the Dowager Augusta, during the wife selection process of Charlotte for King George III. Earl Bute had also served as a powerful diplomat to negotiate the peace agreement with France, that ended the 'Seven Years War.'

Queen of Botany

Bute served as Prime Minister of England; and the First Prime Minister of Scotland. He was disliked by many British, since was a key advisor to King George III, during the American Revolution, when the colonies revolted and Britain lost the war. [174] Bute was blamed alongside the King, for not only losing the war, but losing the slaves and valuable land in the Americas, which had been owned by the British Colonies.

Lord Bute's Botany Books in Charlotte's Wood Cabinet[175]

      For a short time, in addition to his other pursuits, Bute was director of the Kew Gardens. In 1784, he published several books with botanical tables titled *"Botanical Tables Containing the Families of British Plants,* in 1785."[176] Out of high regard for Queen Charlotte, Bute dedicated his books to her to salute her expertise in botany and to praise her support of young ladies and girls who wanted to study botany.

      Queen Charlotte's support for young women botanists was significant because traditional British custom prohibited women from studying academic topics, like botany.[177] Earl Bute probably learned from Charlotte's example that women could be knowledgeable in botany, astronomy and other fields. In his book dedication, Bute acknowledged his recognition of the desire of girls to learn botany. He had observed Charlotte's love of botany from her adolescence to adulthood, and was impressed with her growth of knowledge. His dedication read, "composed solely for the Amusement of the Fair Sex under the Protection of your [Queen Charlotte] Royal Name."[178]

      The Queen received Earl Bute's dedication graciously stating, "…much flattered to be thought capable of so rational, beautiful, & enticing Amusement, & shall make it my endeavor not to forfeit this good opinion by pursuing this

CHAPTER NINE
Queen of Botany

Study steadily, as I am persuaded this Botanical Book will more than encourage me in doing it." Queen Charlotte carefully stored the nine volumes of Earl Bute's books in an elegant satinwood cabinet mounted with gilt bronze handles. A set of Bute's Botanical books are at the National Museum in Wales. [179] Earl Bute gave copies of his illustrated book to some of the most powerful women of his day, including Queen Charlotte; Catherine II, Empress of Russia; Margaret Cavendish Bentinck, The Duchess of Portland; and Mrs. Jane Barrington. He also gave a copy to Sir Joseph Banks.

Needlework and Mosaics

In 1776, her friend the Duchess of Portland introduced Charlotte to Mrs. Delany, a respected painter and embroiderer. At the age of 74, Mrs. Delany had invented a method of cutting out beautiful and decorative paper flowers and plants. Sir Joseph Banks thought Mrs. Delany's paper flowers were true to nature, and found her work so perfect he said he could use her "imitations of nature" to describe a plant botanically, without any fear of error. When Charlotte met Mrs. Delany she was anxious to see a paper mosaic collection Mrs. Delany had designed called, "Flora." [180]

Mary Delany made flowers from cut and colored papers, 1775[181]

In a book *titled, Royal Friendships: The Story of Two Royal Friendships as Derived from histories, diaries, biographies, letters, etc.,* Mrs. Delany describes her first meeting with Queen Charlotte. She writes, "The King desired me to show the Queen one of my books of plants. She seated herself in the gallery; a table and the book laid before her. I kept my distance till she called me to ask some questions about the mosaic paperwork, and as I stood before Her Majesty the King set a chair behind me. I turned with some confusion and hesitation on receiving so great an honor, when the Queen said—'Mrs. Delany, sit down, sit down; it is not every lady that has a chair brought her by a King.' So, I obeyed."[182]

Mrs. Delany did not have many personal financial resources and sadly, one day she found herself homeless, due to the death of the person she was living with. Out of their concern, King George and Queen Charlotte offered Mrs. Delany residence in a small house, at Windsor Castle and provided her with an allowance to help maintain the house. The Queen wrote, "I hope, and add that I shall be extremely glad and happy to see so amiable an inhabitant in this our sweet retreat; and wish very sincerely that my dear Mrs. Delany may enjoy every blessing amongst us that her merits deserve, that we may long enjoy her amiable company. Amen. These are the true sentiments of her very affectionate Queen, — Charlotte." The Royal family enjoyed Mrs. Delany's "amiable company" until the old lady passed away in 1788. Losing Mrs. Delany as a friend and confident was tough on Charlotte since they had become very close and Mrs. Delany's friendship was a source of support—particularly during the turbulent times of the American Revolution, loss of the colonies and the painful onset of the King's illness.[183]

Prince Charles Becomes Patron of Kew Gardens

The historic importance of the Kew Gardens was recognized on July 26, 2016, when Princes Charles, of the British Royal Family became Patron of the Royal Botanic Gardens at Kew. Prince Charles said, "I have always had the greatest affection and admiration for the Royal Botanic Gardens at Kew, so I could not be more proud and delighted to have been invited to become Patron of this great institution." The Prince acknowledged the historic origins of Kew, "Kew has had its roots planted deeply in British soil for more than 250 years, but has developed an international reputation as one of the world's greatest botanic gardens, renowned for its scientific research and plant collections." [184] While the Prince did not mention Queen Charlotte by name it was her work that he referred to that began 250 years ago.

Richard Deverell, director of the Kew Gardens said, "It is a truly great honor to welcome The Prince as our Patron and we look forward to sharing our many exciting plans for a future in which Kew plays a very central role in the conservation and sustainability of our precious planet." [185] In the past, Prince Charles has spoken out on climate change and global warming and clearly inherited the mission of his ancestors in protecting the environment. The Kew website indicates that plans at the Kew Gardens include a 'Great Broad Walk Borders' that will stress the vital role of protecting "unique plants" of the world from extinction. Prince Charles added, "The new Great Broad Walk Borders are a great way to celebrate the diversity of the plant kingdom in all its astonishing richness - particularly at a time when, as scientists at Kew have recently stressed, so many of the world's unique plants are under constant threat of extinction. I very much hope that the new borders will attract even more visitors and encourage them to learn about Kew's exciting role at the heart of global efforts to unlock why plants matter."[186]

CHAPTER TEN
Diplomat and Queen

As Queen of England, Charlotte regularly received Heads of State at the Court, and interacted with foreign dignitaries by letter. The Royal couple hosted countless formal receptions at the Court of St. James and Buckingham Palace for leaders from Europe, Asia, and India. After the American Revolutionary War when peace was negotiated between the newly freed colonies and Britain, the Queen and King George III interacted with several of the founding fathers, of the new United States of America, including Ambassadors John Adams, and Thomas Jefferson.

Pen Pal with Marie Antoinette

One of the Royal leaders Queen Charlotte corresponded with was Queen Marie Antoinette of France. They were both a key part of major families who presided over not only their nations but, colonies around the world. Charlotte and Marie Antoinette exchanged letters about their love of music and art and shared information about the major political upheavals they faced during the 1770's and 80's. Along with her husband King George III, Charlotte experienced trauma during the American Revolution in the 1760's and Marie Antoinette suffered the loss of her throne, through the French Revolution of 1789.

While there is no record of Queen Charlotte and Queen Marie Antoinette ever meeting face to face, their active correspondence addressed many vital issues. For example, when the French Revolution broke out, Marie Antoinette confided in Charlotte that she was afraid and might have to leave France. Charlotte responded by inviting Marie and the Royal family of France to escape to England, but Marie Antoinette didn't move fast enough and the rebels in France took over the government. Charlotte was horrified when she learned Marie Antoinette had been executed.

CHAPTER TEN
Diplomat and Queen

Hosted John and Abigail Adams

After the American colonies won the Revolutionary War against the British empire, the new American government sought diplomatic recognition from England. In 1785, eight years after the end of the Revolutionary War, John and Abigail Adams went to the British Court to be received by King George III

and Queen Charlotte. It was a tense meeting since the colonies had rebelled but, as America's first official Ambassador to England, Adams wanted to be received at the court by the King and Queen. This level of reception would prove to the world that America was a sovereign nation.

John and Abigail Adams Waited 2 Hours to be Received by Queen Charlotte

After their visit to the Royal Court, Abigail Adams wrote a letter to her sister describing their reception, that included observations about Queen Charlotte. Abigail Adams wrote, "At two o'clock we went to the circle, which is in the drawing-room of the Queen…We were placed in a circle round the drawing-room, which was very full, I believe two hundred persons present. Only think of the task! The Royal family have to go round to every person, and find small talk enough to speak to all of them, though they very prudently speak in a whisper so, that only the person who stands next to you can hear what is said. The King enters the room and goes round to the right, the Queen and Princesses to the left… The King is a personable man, but, my dear sister, he has a certain countenance, which you and I have often remarked; a red face and white eyebrows. The Queen has a similar countenance…Persons are not placed according to their rank in the drawing-room, but promiscuously…It was more than two hours after this before it came to my turn to be presented to the Queen."

Abigail was clearly frustrated by standing so long to be received by the Royal couple. She continued, "The circle was so large that the company was four hours standing… the manner, in which they make their tour round the room, is, first, the Queen, the lady in waiting behind her, holding up her train; next to her, the Princess Royal; after her, Princess Augusta, and their lady in waiting behind them. They are pretty, rather than beautiful, well-shaped, with fair complexions, and a tincture of the King's countenance. The Queen was in purple and silver. She is not well shaped, nor handsome." [187]   References to the Queen not being "handsome" may have been references to Charlotte's Moorish or Negroid facial features.

On another occasion, Abigail, John Adams and their daughter Nabby went to St James Palace for Queen Charlotte's 42nd birthday. According to Nabby they "pushed their way through the great crush of well-wishers and situated ourselves so, that the King spoke to us very soon." It took longer for them to get to the Queen, but after they paid their respects they left the palace since they knew they would have to return to the Queen's ball that evening. [188]   It was clear from these reports that the Adams family knew Queen Charlotte was in charge, and American diplomats had to wait their turn.

Thomas Jefferson

Before he became President of the United States Thomas Jefferson, a leader of the American Revolutionary War, went to England to serve as a diplomat with John Adams. While there in 1786, he was received by King George III at the Court of St. James, as an official representative of the newly minted nation called the United States of America. Jefferson attended a number of receptions at the Court of St. James and Buckingham Palace, where he was received by Queen Charlotte. In 1787, a year after Jefferson arrived in England, his teenage daughter Mary Jefferson, came to London, accompanied by an enslaved young mulatto girl named Sally Hemmings. Both girls stayed in London for two weeks at the home of John and Abigail Adams. [189] It is not known if Sally Hemmings or Jefferson's daughter Mary were received by Queen Charlotte at the British Court but, it would not have been unusual if they had visited the Court. During the time he stayed in Europe, Thomas Jefferson developed a personal relationship with his daughter's maid, Sally Hemmings. In later years, he had mixed race children with Sally Hemmings at his plantation at Monticello, in Charlottesville, Virginia. Note, Charlottesville, Virginia, is named for Queen Charlotte.

During his stay in England, Thomas Jefferson and Queen Charlotte became friends. On May 12, 1806, after he became U.S. President, Jefferson wrote a letter to the Queen to introduce her to two new diplomats—James Monroe and William

Pinkney. They were coming to England from America, and Jefferson wanted them to meet her and the King. An indication of the friendly relationship between President Jefferson and Charlotte is noted where Jefferson, refers to Queen Charlotte as "My Friend." (see text of letter)[190] One might wonder if Jefferson recognized Charlotte's mixed-race features since he fathered five (5) mixed race children with Sally Hemmings. When Jefferson returned to Virginia, he became President of the United States and continued to write Charlotte letters. One of the letters is displayed here.

Thomas Jefferson's Letter to Queen Charlotte
FROM THOMAS JEFFERSON TO CHARLOTTE SOPHIA, 12 MAY 1806

12 MAY 1806

MADAM, OUR GOOD FRIEND,

I have named JAMES MONROE and WILLIAM PINKNEY, Commissioners Plenipotentiary and Extraordinary of the United States of America to your Royal Consort. My knowledge of their good qualities gives me full confidence that they will so conduct themselves as to merit your esteem. I pray, therefore, that you yield entire Credence to the assurances which they will bear to you of our friendship; And that God may always have you, Madam, our Good Friend, in his holy keeping.

Written at the City of Washington the Twelfth day of May in the year of our Lord one thousand eight hundred and six.

Your Good Friend,

TH: JEFFERSON
By the President
JAMES MADISON
Secretary of State.[191]

CHAPTER TEN
Diplomat and Queen

Benjamin Franklin

There is no record that Benjamin Franklin, signer of the Declaration of Independence, statesman, author, publisher, scientist, inventor and diplomat ever personally met Queen Charlotte. However, sometime during 1772, Franklin gave a swath of silk fabric to his friend Sir John Pringle, Charlotte's physician, to give to the Queen. In a note to Sir John Pringle Franklin wrote, "Dr. F. presents his respectful Compliments to Sir J. Pringle, is much oblig'd to him for the Trouble he has so kindly taken in the Affair of the Silk, and is very happy to learn that the Queen has graciously condescended to accept it with a Purpose of wearing it. Her Majesty's Countenance so afforded to the Raisers of Silk in Pennsylvania (where her Character is highly rever'd) will give them great Encouragement to proceed in a Measure the British Parliament seems to have had much at Heart, the Procuring a Supply of that valuable Article from our Colonies, for which at present large Sums are paid yearly to France, Spain, Italy and the Indies." [192] Reports indicate that Queen had the silk fabric made into a beautiful gown.

Nawab Muhammad Ali Khan Wala-Jah, Ruler in India

Other diplomats Queen Charlotte and King George III interacted with were leaders from India. One leader was Nawab Muhammad Ali Khan Wala-Jah, an Indian ruler, who was their ally with the East Indian Trading Company. Nawab

Muhammad Ali Khan-Wala owed the British for restoration of his throne and maintenance of his kingdom, and he was grateful to the British couple. Based on historical records in the India Records Archive, he wrote many letters to George III and Queen Charlotte, from 1760-1784, about working closely together, trying to control trade and his dislike of certain British officials.

Nawab Muhammad Ali Khan Wala-Jah, ruler of India, [193]

CHAPTER TEN
Diplomat and Queen

One story tells about Muhammad Ali Khan Wala-Jah who wrote a letter October 7, 1771, to Queen Charlotte where he described the final hours and death of his beloved wife, Nawab Begum, who suffered from a long illness. On her death bed, her Highness Nawab Begum urged her husband and their children to maintain their carefully cultivated friendship with the British people. Nawab Muhammad wrote that his wife wanted to "be personally remembered" by Queen Charlotte," and that she had asked him to give Charlotte some of her own personal jewels. [194]

Queen Charlotte wearing "Arcot Diamonds." Portrait by Esther Denner, 1861

Nawab Muhammad Ali Khan wrote that he was sending Charlotte "a cluster consisting of a brilliant set, round with other diamonds, cut & polished after the manner of this country, with a polished emerald drop scallop'd on the surface and the edge."[195] The gift was two beautiful Arcot diamonds that Charlotte had made into earrings, and wore to formal affairs. According to the website www.internetstones.com, "Queen Charlotte was famous for superbly bejewelling herself while at Court or for formal state occasions."[196] The portrait of Queen Charlotte above shows her wearing the drop earrings she had made and hair ornaments with at least two drop-shaped diamonds and a collar brooch, with at least three drop-shaped diamonds. The diamonds matched each other in size and shape and one was estimated to be 33.70 karats and the smaller diamond 23.65 karats. Charlotte wore the "Arcot Diamonds" throughout her lifetime and left them in her will to her daughters and granddaughters.[197]

CHAPTER ELEVEN
Faith, Philanthropy, Hospitals and Pets

Queen Charlotte supported charities consistent with her faith and her desire to help others. She helped orphanages, homes for homeless musicians, advocated on behalf of enslaved people and provided services for poor families who relied on her patronage. As the Queen quietly moved through England, to help the underprivileged some writers believe she went "undercover" into community settings in poor neighborhoods of London, where slaves and poor whites lived so, she wouldn't be recognized.

Her sense of civic responsibility began as a youth when she attended the Herford Ministry in Germany, and was made a Canoness of the church. While a student there Charlotte learned core religious principles and she stayed close to her faith throughout her life and taught her children faith in God. According to the 1829 book "A Brief Memoir of Her Majesty Queen Charlotte" by Thomas Williams, "her Majesty always set a laudable example by her attendance upon public worship."[198] She attended church regularly and interacted with religious leaders on behalf of herself, and her husband King George III and prayed constantly that her beloved husband would recover from his severe illness.

In a letter to her brother dated November 8, 1172, Charlotte wrote about her faith, *"Sir, my dearest brother. A thousand thanks for the book of Mr. Gellert. I believe if there ever was a saint on this earth it would have to be him. The greatest libertine could not read this book without becoming good himself, and what effect it must have on those who contemplate it deeply……each time I read his Moral Writings and Spiritual Odes my Christian faith reaffirms itself. The fear and terror at the approach of his death and yet his trust in God are exquisitely beautiful. The advice he gives to his discouraged friend with the comforting words: Rejoice, and again I say to you Rejoice! is so encouraging and so comforting and so exciting that I might almost say that after reading it I thought of myself of being in higher and better worlds than the moment I now worry about. Alas, how many unrecognized blessings do we not all enjoy in our appointed station? I wished I would be able to recognize mine, but that degree of*

Faith, Philanthropy, Hospitals and Pets

perfection I have not been able to obtain, being quite human. I am hopeful, however, that with God's help I shall gain a good conscience. To my infinite consolation, there is a contentment which the world can neither give nor take away from me. I assure you on my honor, dear brother, that each day I pass in this world, I discover, little by little, that the Royal Crown and the title of Majesty do not bear comparison with that of a Christian. The latter not only furnishes me with but also commands me to fulfil the duties of humanity."

Charlotte[199]

Queen Charlotte's Lying-In Hospital

Queen Charlotte and Chelsea Hospital Mail Building, United Kingdom

Before Charlotte moved to England, from Germany, in 1739, Sir Richard Manningham founded a hospital of lying-in-beds in a 17-room house in England.[200] In 1752, it evolved to a medical facility known as the "Lying-In-Hospital." The Lying-In Hospital was a place where poor women could give birth to their children, since prior to 1752, there were no medical charities in London for poor pregnant women. Thousands of British, Scottish and Irish poor women had to give birth at home in places described as "...damp cellars subject to floods from excessive rain; destitute of attendance, medicine, and often of proper food, by which hundreds perished with their little infants."[201] After she moved to England and became mother of 15 children, Queen Charlotte learned how complicated childbirth could be. While she was fortunate to have Court Physicians, midwives and other to help her she knew that poor women didn't have any of those resources. When Charlotte learned about the Lying-In Hospitals, she made donations and provided support that enabled the hospitals to start "Midwife" training programs that provided services to 4,000 poor women.

SAVE THE CHILDREN.

Queen Charlotte's Maternity Hospital

(Formerly Queen Charlotte's Lying-in Hospital.)

Founded 1739.

MARYLEBONE ROAD, N.W.1.

Receives 2,000 POOR WOMEN into the Wards annually and attends over 2,000 OTHERS in their own homes. £250,000 urgently required for Rebuilding the Hospital, for Research and for Partial Endowment.

ARTHUR WATTS, Secretary.

Queen Charlotte's Maternity Hospital, Kilburn, England, 1931

In 1784, a formal petition was sent to Her Majesty the Queen to grant a Charter of Incorporation for a Hospital that would have her name on it. She agreed and the group of hospitals became known as, "Queen Charlotte's Lying-In Hospital." Over time, the hospital moved from location to location but, it still exists today in London, with the name Chelsea Hospital. In 1885, author Thomas Ryan wrote a book about Queen Charlotte's Lying-In Hospital. (available via archive in PDF.) [202] Queen Charlotte's role in providing safe, medical environments for women to have their children is indisputable and was a major contribution to women's health in London, and in the world. Hospitals named 'Queen Charlotte's Maternity Hospital' still exist today in parts of England.

CHAPTER ELEVEN
Faith, Philanthropy, Hospitals and Pets

Pet Lover

Queen Charlotte loved pets. When she traveled to England to marry King George III, she brought her two dogs with her.[203] Her dogs, called "wolf dogs" were mainly white in color and were bred in Pomerania, Germany, a region along the southern Baltic coast near Charlotte's home of Mecklenburg.[204] Queen Charlotte referred to the breed as "The Pomeranian," and that name stuck until modern times. The Pomerian dogs were small and compact with a dense, double coat of long hairs, soft wooly undercoat, and flat tails. Charlotte's dogs were named Phoebe and Mercury.

Charlotte with her Pomeranian Dog, by Sir Thomas Gainsborough[205]

Charlotte's love of dogs was passed down to her granddaughter Queen Victoria who made the Pomeranian dog, a very popular breed. Victoria traveled with her dogs on overseas trips and had special compartments built to house them on Royal trains. Queen Victoria's dogs were so special they had their own policemen to ensure their safety and security. Victoria's favorite Pomeranian was named "Marco." Sir Thomas Gainsborough, painted a portrait of Queen Charlotte with her favorite dog.

CHAPTER ELEVEN
Faith, Philanthropy, Hospitals and Pets

Needlework

Queen Charlotte excelled at needlework and embroidery. She personally sewed clothes and took a keen interest in how designers created stylish gowns and outfits. She closely monitored the cotton trade as it grew worldwide, and was a customer of fine linen fabrics from the Scottish cities of Glasgow and Paisley. Charlotte monitored how the Scottish manufacturers became involved with Indian looms that produced beautiful cotton linens. She learned about cottons from a Scottish artisan named James Monteith, of Glasgow, who worked with the Indians from India, who were expert on the looms and produced the first muslin woven in Scotland, from Indian yarn.

Monteith was so successful at producing muslin fabrics, that he made a beautiful dress out of linen, with gold embroidery and presented it to Queen Charlotte in 1793. [206] This was around the same time the "spinning-mule" or "spinning-wheel" was invented. The timing of the invention of the spinning-wheel was discussed in a report by the directors of the East India Company as an asset to the future of cotton manufacturing.[207] Charlotte's interest in fabric and her understanding of designing clothes contributed to a national interest in the spinning wheel.

Unfortunately, there was a tragic outcome in how the growing worldwide interest in cotton contributed to the expansion of the Trans-Atlantic slave trade-- particularly in North America. As cotton became a major trading product, plantation owners increased their demand for enslaved workers to produce the cotton and there was increased demand for millions of African people to be kidnapped and sold into slavery, to grow cotton in the southern states of America. The author did not discover if Queen Charlotte made the connection between how cotton promoted slavery the way she realized how sugar promoted slavery. Information is not available about whether Charlotte protested the expansion of the cotton industry, like the way she protested the sugar-saccharine industry, in collaboration Granville Sharp and William Wilberforce.

Wright School of Embroidery

Queen Charlotte was particularly concerned about young women in England, who needed assistance due to the death of their fathers, or both parents. In the late 1700's and early 1800's, there was no welfare system, food stamps, foster care or subsidized housing in England, to help care for girls who didn't have fathers, brothers or mothers. When their parents died, the young girls were entirely dependent on extended families or, were forced into labor at very young ages—often in difficult and abusive circumstances. In 1772, the Queen heard about several young women from respectable families whose fathers had died or gone bankrupt and she became very concerned about their welfare.

Charlotte's official State Bed, embroidered by girls from Wright School of Embroidery[208]

Out of concern for the needy girls in London, Queen Charlotte approached Phoebe Wright, a woman who served in her Court as a professional embroiderer and owned a popular embroidery shop in London. Charlotte knew Mrs. Wright well since her shop provided embroidery for Buckingham Palace, Windsor Castle and the Queens Cottage at Kew and Frogmore. The Queen asked Mrs. Wright if she would take in indigent girls and teach them basic manners, reading, writing and how to become professional embroiderers. Since Mrs. Wright was an older woman and didn't have children in her household, she agreed to try.

To assist her with the effort, Queen Charlotte donated 500 British pounds per year to the new embroidery school. Her donation in 1774 based on 2014 U.S. dollars would have been approximately $ 21,200.00 annually. In addition to her financial donations, Charlotte paid the girls professional fees for their work at the Royal palaces and castles. For example, in the 1790s Queen Charlotte gave her decorator Mary Moser, a prestigious commission to design a decorative floral scheme for Frogmore House, that included a design for the official state bed. But, the design Mary Moser developed required over 4,000 botanically accurate embroidered flowers and she needed help to produce that many flowers. So, the Queen paid the Wright School girls to embroider the fabric to make the 4,000 flowers. Although the bed was never slept in, the beautiful spread and canopy were used as displays of the exquisite needlework produced by the orphaned girls, who lived at the Wright School of Embroidery.[209]

The Queen not only donated money to the Wright School for Embroidery but, she visited the school regularly and got to know the girls by name. Her patronage encouraged other members of the wealthy British aristocracy to buy the girls' embroidery products, and this expanded their customer base. In addition to basic education, the Wright School girls learned complex Continental and French stitches of embroidery, linen weaving and how to work with lush velvets and fine fabrics.[210] Queen Charlotte's involvement and support for the Wright school spanned over 46 years, from 1772, until the school closed in 1818.[211] Hundreds of girls were helped by Queen Charlotte's compassion and the Wright School.

Lodging for Elders

Another charity of Queen Charlotte's was Bailbrook Lodge. It was a facility near Bath, England, that provided residential housing for older ladies of respectable character who were homeless, due to no fault of their own. Unfortunately, even though Bailbrook Lodge had the support of the Queen it failed after a year, because the senior women couldn't get along with each other. Instead, the Bailbrook Lodge became a hotel where the Queen and other aristocrats went to take advantage of the healthy waters.

William Wilberforce, a member of the British Parliament and famed abolitionist, was one of the guests who frequented Bailbrook Lodge and during his visits he and the Queen may have had private opportunities to discuss their opposition to slavery and what the abolitionist movement was doing in England and in the colonies. Perhaps the discussions between the Queen and Wilberforce helped to plan strategy that King George used with the Parliament, to oppose slavery. Finally, in 1808 the Parliament did abolish slavery in England, and the actions of Parliament were largely based on Wilberforce's decades long advocacy. England ended slavery 55 years before the United States Congress and President Abraham Lincoln abolished slavery in the United States, after the Civil War.

Faith, Philanthropy, Hospitals and Pets

Queen Charlotte as Publisher

In addition to enjoying reading, Queen Charlotte printed and published her own books. Ellis Cornelia Knight, a member of Charlotte's Royal household and her librarian, Edward Harding, were instrumental in working with her to set up a private press, at Frogmore. The Queen's extensive library occupied the pavilion, at the southern end of the country estate. There was a back door in the library that led into the room where Queen Charlotte kept her botanical collections, her printing press, and more books. Among the items found in her library was a book about one of her favorite herbariums, written by her friend Reverend John Lightfoot, who taught her botany before he died.

Books produced by the Queen's printing press were given away by Charlotte as gifts. Some of the books were produced on cards, rather than printed with book binding. Examples of book-cards produced by the Queen's printing press were: Translations from the German in Prose and Verse; Miscellaneous Poems; A Chronological Abridgement of the History of Spain, on cards, Windsor, 1809; A Chronological Abridgement of the History of Germany, on cards, Windsor, 1810; A Chronological Abridgement of the History of France, on cards. (Windsor, 1811) A Chronological Abridgement of the History of Portugal, on cards (Windsor, 1817); and A Chronological Abridgement of the History of Ancient Rome, on cards Windsor, 1817.

For more information about the Queen's Library, with illustrations, and more on her collections and pastimes with her daughters, readers can read a book by W. H. Pyne, titled *The History of the Royal Residences of Windsor Castle, St. James's Palace, Carlton House, Kensington Palace, Hampton Court, Buckingham House and Frogmore* (London, 1819.). Unfortunately, most of Charlotte's personal library was sold in 1819, after her death for the financial benefit of her children. Although the collection was dispersed, there is a sales catalog that gives a good idea of what Charlotte owned titled, "A Catalogue of the Genuine Library, Prints and Books of Prints of an Illustrious Personage," Christies, London, 9 June–16 July 1819. [212]

CHAPTER TWELVE
Mozart, Pudding, Painting and Christmas Trees

King George III and Queen Charlotte loved music and supported composers who became legends in music. One of the talented composers who worked with them was Johann Christian Bach, son of famous composer Johann Sebastian Bach. In 1762, Bach became a composer at the King's Theatre in London, where he wrote several successful Italian operas. He also received a lucrative appointment as music master to Queen Charlotte and her children, and was a social and musical success.[213]

Author Olwen Hedley reported that King George and Queen Charlotte were patrons of the Theatre Royal in High Street, near Windsor Palace, where they enjoyed many uproarious evenings with their neighbors, who lived near the Palace. Queen Charlotte and King George III had front row boxes for themselves and their family, and loudly laughed at the frolics of famous actors, actresses, and comedians. The theater events were heralded by Charles Knight, a member of the Royal entourage as 'the heyday of the old uninhibited fellowship between monarchy and the masses.'[214] The Royal couple also had concerts with their children every evening in their Music Room at Windsor Palace, after which they played backgammon and other card games.[215] Charlotte enjoyed these festivities and added fireworks displays and elaborate festivals of art, music events and concerts.

Discovering Mozart

One musical genius that Charlotte supported was Wolfgang Amadeus Mozart. When he was only 8 years old, Wolfgang and his family visited Britain. It was during April 1764, when his family was making a grand tour of Europe to introduce his musical talents to potential sponsors. They were invited to the Court for an audition and young Mozart played for the Queen and her music teacher Johann Christian Bach. During the audition, Bach tested young Mozart's skills

Mozart, Pudding, Painting and Christmas Trees

by putting difficult works of Handel, J. S. Bach, and Carl Friedrich Abel before him and asking him to play them. Young Wolfgang impressed the Queen, Bach and the entire Court when he played all of the music they provided.

Amadeus Mozart, (1763). Portrait ascribed to Pietro Antonio Lorenzoni [216]

After his audition, young Mozart accompanied the Queen, as she sang an aria. He also played a solo work on the flute. He quickly became a favorite of the Court and with the Queen's approval, Johann Christian Bach became Wolfgang's mentor and helped him to develop his historic musical career.[217] When Mozart composed "Mozart's Opus 3," a series of six sonatas, that were published in London, he dedicated them to Queen Charlotte. [218] As a reward, Queen Charlotte presented him with 50 guinea coins--each coin was worth 22 karats in gold. Note: King George III had gold guineas minted between 1761-1799, as the major British coin of the eighteenth century. The gold for the coin was supplied by the Africa Company operating along the Guinea Coast, of Africa, and was undoubtedly connected to the slave trade.[219] When Queen Charlotte gave Mozart fifty guinea coins worth 22 karats each, the value was approximately $16,000 based on the value of gold in Y'2016. This demonstrated the high-value Queen Charlotte placed on supporting artists, musicians, and writers. In addition to Johann Christian Bach and Wolfgang Amadeus Mozart, Queen Charlotte was also a passionate admirer of the music of George Frederic Handel.

Mozart, Pudding, Painting and Christmas Trees

Patron of Black Violinist

George Augustus Polgreen Bridgtower, picture by Henry Edridge, 1790[220]

In 1779, a musical prodigy named George Augustus Polgreen Bridgtower was born to an African man named John Frederick Bridgtower, and his wife Maria, a Polish woman. Young Bridgtower was an amazing violinist at an early age, who created excitement throughout London. Queen Charlotte invited George Bridgtower to play at one of their regular concerts at Windsor Place. It was bold for King George and Queen Charlotte to host a young Black man like Bridgtower since the slave trade was operating at an intense level and African people were being oppressed all over the world. Their support for Bridgtower showed that they were trying to overcome racial boundaries to showcase the talent of a young musical genius.

According to Mrs. Papendiek, Assistant Keeper of the Wardrobe to Queen Charlotte the young violinist Bridgtower was, "a most prepossessing lad of ten years old, and a fine violin player." The Queen agreed and as his patron she introduced him to the British cultural community. As Bridgtower grew older he became known within musical circles and became close friends with the famous composer Ludwig van Beethoven. Bridgtower, the mixed-race son of an African and Polish couple, was fortunate to have Queen Charlotte and her family among his patrons.[221]

Charlotte Russe Dessert

A desert pudding named after Queen Charlotte, became popular in America and Europe, during the last part of the 18th century. "Charlottes" as the pudding was known as, were invented in England and tasted like bread pudding. Throughout Europe fancy, apple, apricot and pear molded desserts remained popular through the 19th and 20th centuries. In modern times, another version of the dessert was called "Charlotte Russe," and is made with cream, instead of fruit. The popular confections ultimately inspired the Brooklyn New York legendary

Mozart, Pudding, Painting and Christmas Trees

childhood bakery staple called "Charley Roosh." People who grew up in New York know the "Charley Roosh" dessert well, even today.[222]

Recipe for Charlotte Russe

Ingredients
1 envelope unflavored gelatin
1/2 cup cold water
5 large egg yolks
1 1/2 cups sugar
2 teaspoons all-purpose flour
1/2 teaspoon table salt
2 cups Mocha Mix
1 teaspoon vanilla extract
1/2 cup Cooking Sherry (non-alcohol)
2 (3.5-oz.) packages hard ladyfingers
2 cups heavy cream
Spread whip cream on top

Preparation

1. Sprinkle gelatin over 1/2 cup cold water; stir and let stand 5 minutes. Whisk together egg yolks and next 3 ingredients in a bowl.
2. Bring half-and-half to a simmer in a medium saucepan over medium heat. Whisk 1/4 cup hot half-and-half into egg mixture; add egg mixture to remaining hot half-and-half, whisking constantly. Reduce heat to medium-low, and cook, stirring constantly, 8 to 10 minutes or until mixture thickens and coats a spoon. Add vanilla, gelatin mixture, and 1/4 cup sherry, stirring until combined.
3. Remove from heat; let stand 15 minutes. Transfer to a bowl. Cover and chill 2 hours or until mixture is a pudding-like thickness, stirring every 30 minutes.
4. Arrange 23 ladyfingers in a single layer on a jelly-roll pan. Brush both sides of ladyfingers with remaining 1/4 cup cooking sherry.
5. Line a 9-cup charlotte mold or soufflé dish with plastic wrap, allowing 2 to 3 inches to extend over sides. Line sides of the mold with ladyfingers.
6. Beat cream at medium speed with a heavy-duty electric stand mixer 2 to 3 minutes or until soft peaks form. Fold whipped cream into chilled half-and-half mixture. Gently pour mixture into prepared charlotte mold. Cover and chill 8 to 24 hours or until fully set. To unmold, invert a flat plate over dessert. Holding containers together, invert. Lift off mold, and gently remove plastic wrap. Garnish as desired. Cut dessert into wedges.[223]

CHAPTER TWELVE
Mozart, Pudding, Painting and Christmas Trees

Popularization of the Christmas Tree

Decorated Christmas Trees are among the most popular items of the Christmas season, in Europe and America. But, how did Christmas Trees become popular? When researching the background of the Christmas Tree one learns that Charlotte's hometown of Mirow, Germany, was near the community where Martin Luther, the father of the Lutheran religion lived. Martin Luther is credited with being the first to use fir branches and fir trees as decorative items, sometime during 1536. Over the centuries, the fir tree came to be known as the holiday Christmas Tree. As the story goes, Martin Luther was walking through a pine forest near his home in Wittenberg, Germany, on an evening when there were thousands of stars glinting in the sky. The beautiful sight of stars glittering among the branches of the trees inspired him to set up a candle-lit fir tree in his house that would remind his children of the starry heavens from whence the Savior Jesus Christ came. From that date forward, the Christmas Tree became an important part of celebrating the birth of Jesus Christ and Christianity. The tradition of making trees the centerpiece of the Christian Christmas Holiday continued in southern Germany and by 1605, Germans started decorated Christmas Trees by setting up box trees, fir trees and yews in their parlors. Charlotte grew up with this tradition in her hometown of Mirow, where it was the custom to deck out a single yew branch from evergreen trees and shrubs that came from Europe, North America, and Japan.[224]

The website, "History Today" produced by History Today Ltd., reports that "Prince Albert, Queen Victoria's consort, is usually credited with having introduced the Christmas Tree into England in 1840. However, this author disagrees since history shows the tradition of the Christmas tree started in Germany decades earlier. In fact, as the story will show credit for establishing the Christmas tree as a tradition in the United Kingdom, rightfully belongs to Queen Charlotte. She set up the first known decorated Christmas tree at Queen's Lodge, Windsor, in December 1800." [225]

Fir Trees used to Celebrate the Christian Christmas Holiday

In 1798, a poet named Samuel Taylor Coleridge visited Charlotte's home region in Mecklenburg-Strelitz and was struck by the yew-branch ceremony held during Christmas. He saw that Charlotte had been raised in a culture that

Mozart, Pudding, Painting and Christmas Trees

decorated yew branches and exchanged gifts for Christmas. Colenridge believed Charlotte took the custom to England with her. In a letter to his wife April 23, 1799, Coleridge wrote about a Christmas celebration at one of the Royal palaces. He wrote, "On the evening before Christmas Day, one of the parlors is lighted up by the children, into which the parents must not go; a great yew bough is fastened on the table at a little distance from the wall, a multitude of little tapers are fixed in the bough ... and colored paper etc. hangs and flutters from the twigs. Under this bough the children lay out the presents they mean for their parents, still concealing in their pockets what they intend for each other. Then the parents are introduced, and each presents his little gift; they then bring out the remainder one by one from their pockets, and present them with kisses and embraces." [226]

Brooch of Queen Charlotte, by J.H. Hurter, 1781

When Queen Charlotte gave parties at the English court for Christmas, she transformed the private yew-branch ritual into a more public celebration enjoyed by her family, their friends and all the members of the Royal household. She placed yew branches in the largest rooms at Kew Palace and Windsor Castle and with assistance from her Ladies-In-Waiting she decorated branches with candles and other ornaments. When all the wax tapers were lit, the whole Court gathered round and sang carols. The festivity ended with a distribution of gifts which included such items as clothes, jewels, plate, toys, and sweets.

The practice of decorating yew branches at court caused quite a stir among the nobility, who had never seen anything like it. But it was nothing to the sensation created in 1800 when Queen Charlotte set-up the first real English Christmas tree at a Christmas party for the children of all the principal families in Windsor. She gave the children a special treat and decided that instead of the customary yew bough, she put up an entire yew tree. Queen Charlotte got personally involved with covering the tree with baubles and fruit and loading it with presents. Then she had the tree set up in the middle of the drawing-room

Mozart, Pudding, Painting and Christmas Trees

floor at Queen's Lodge with brilliant decorations. She believed the decorated fir tree would be enchanting for the children to gaze upon. She was right—they loved it and still love it today.

Dr. John Watkins, one of Queen Charlotte's biographers who attended the Christmas party at Queens Lodge, at Windsor wrote, "In the middle of the room stood an immense tub with a yew tree placed in it, from the branches of which hung bunches of sweetmeats, almonds, and raisins in papers, fruits and toys, most tastefully arranged, and the whole illuminated by small wax candles. After the company had walked around and admired the tree, each child obtained a portion of the sweets which it bore together with a toy and then all returned home, quite delighted."[227] After Charlotte introduced the decorated Christmas tree, it became the rage among the English upper-class and became the center of attention at countless children's gatherings with the trees candle-lit, adorned with trinkets and surrounded by piles of presents.

John Fraser, an adventurer and explorer who brought the Queen fir trees from Cuba and the Americas, discovered fir trees in the Northwest section of America. Today, the trees he found carry the name "Fraser Fir."[228] As a way of imitating the English Christmas tree tradition that Charlotte started, Fraser starting using the "Fraser Fir" as a Christmas tree in the Americas. By 1860, there was scarcely a well-off family in England or America that did not sport Christmas trees in parlors and halls and at holiday parties held for children. Fraser is often incorrectly credited with introducing the Christmas tree to America--that credit properly belongs to Queen Charlotte. She brought the tradition from Mirow, in Mecklenburg, Germany to England and popularized the decorative model of Christmas celebrations with fir trees. Her holiday model is the one that was transferred to the Americas.

In keeping with Queen Charlotte's love for children from all walks of life, special emphasis was placed on gift-laden Christmas trees at events for children, including poor children. Decorated Christmas trees always delight both children and adults alike. But perhaps no tree ever gave greater pleasure than that first magnificent Yuletide tree set up in Windsor Palace by Queen Charlotte for the enjoyment of the local children.[229] Although it is largely unknown, Queen Charlotte is the inventor of the Christmas tree tradition that today flourishes all over the world.

CHAPTER TWELVE
Mozart, Pudding, Painting and Christmas Trees

Personal Painting and Music

In addition to her love of music and art, Queen Charlotte performed and painted pictures. Although it does not appear that any of her personal pictures survived, she did enjoy personal painting. For example, evidence of Charlotte's personal painting hobby was described in a letter she wrote to her brother Adolph, to request help with her painting projects. In her letter to him dated February 23, 1790, she asked her brother to send her paint that she could personally use in her artwork. She wrote, *"Sir, my very dear brother and friend, you have acquitted yourself so well of all the commissions I had assigned you that I feel encouraged to ask you once more. Be assured, at the same time, that I am ready to render the same service to you when you have need of it. It is a matter, dear brother, of procuring paint colors for painting gouache (Note: gouache is a method of painting using opaque pigments ground in water and thickened with a glue-like substance) and I would much prefer to have those from Nuremberg as the place most well-known for this kind of painting. I wish to have one set of colors fully prepared in their manner and another set which can be prepared here. At the same time would it be possible to obtain some information if they use pure water for painting or whether they use gum arabicum water and which make of gum they use for mixing it. Similarly, as they color the prints, whether they first cover the etching with a gum solution before the color is applied or afterwards; whether they use white in the color pigment and by which means do they achieve their nuances, because the way they create the nuances is the major feature of their work. Be so kind as to conceal my name, and to not let this purchase become too expensive; and, if it is possible to obtain all this information before the courier leaves Hanover I believe you are an angel... I love you with all my heart and am until death."*

Your most devoted sister
Charlotte [230]

CHAPTER THIRTEEN
Places Named for Queen Charlotte

There are several cities, counties, ships and objects around the world that are named for Queen Charlotte. Several of the cities were established when she married King George III, and others were established decades and centuries later. Listed below are some of the geographical locations, statues and ships named for Queen Charlotte.

Cities, Towns and Counties (Partial Listing)

(1)   **Queens County, Nova Scotia, Canada.** This area was one of the first places named in honor of the young Queen Charlotte in 1761. T the area was settled in the 18th century by Scottish Highlanders and, after the American Revolution, by Loyalists from the United States, many of whom were runaway slaves, who escaped Plantations for freedom during the American Revolution and relocated in Novia Scotia.

(2)   **Queen Charlotte Islands**, off the northern coast of British Columbia. Juan Pérez was the first European to sight the islands in 1774. They were visited by James Cook in 1778, and named by Captain James Dixon in 1787, after his ship the Queen Charlotte, which was named after Queen Charlotte.

(3)   **Queens College, now named Rutgers University, New Jersey**. On November 10, 1766, William Franklin, the last Colonial governor of New Jersey, signed the charter that brought Queen's College into existence. This new college was named in honor of Queen Charlotte of Mecklenburg. The College changed its name to Rutgers University, November, 1825, in honor of Colonel Henry Rutledge, a hero of the American Revolution.

Places Named for Queen Charlotte

(4) **Charlottesville, Virginia.** This city was named in honor of Princess Charlotte, at the time of her marriage to King George III, in 1761. President Thomas Jefferson lived in Charlottesville.

(5) **Charlotte, North Carolina,** known as "The Queen City" was founded in 1768 and is surrounded by Mecklenburg County, named in honor of Mecklenburg-Strelitz, home of Queen Charlotte. Charlotte, North Carolina is a major U.S. city.

(6) **Camp Charlotte, Ohio.** The first battle in the American Revolutionary War, in 1774, known as the Battle of Point Pleasant. The battle was led by Lord Dunsmore, British Governor of Virginia. His Colonel Andrew Lewis named the camp "Camp Charlotte" in honor of Queen Charlotte.

Historic Marker of Lord Dunsmore's battle.[231]

(7) **Charlotte County, Virginia.** A rural community was established in Virginia in 1764, three years after Charlotte married King George III. Revolutionary War hero Patrick Henry is buried there.

(8) **Charlotte, New York,** is in Chautauqua County, New York.

(9) **Charlotte Neighborhood, Rochester, New York.** This area is located along the western bank of the mouth of the Genesee River along Lake Ontario.

CHAPTER THIRTEEN
Places Named for Queen Charlotte

(10)   **Charlotte, Iowa.** The City of Charlotte is a small, rural city in Eastern Iowa, located in Clinton county. It was founded in 1853, by Albert Gilmore who named the town after his wife, Charlotte. His wife may have been named for Queen Charlotte.

(11)   **Charlotte, Maine**, in Washington County. Named for the wife of a legislator named William Vance, however, she may have been named for Queen Charlotte.

(12)   **Charlotte, Michigan,** originally known as Eaton Center or Carmel, the village of Charlotte was incorporated, on October 12, 1863.

(13)   **Charlotte, Chittenden County, Vermont.** This city was originally named "Charlotta," in honor of Sophia Charlotte of Mecklenburg-Strelitz, shortly after she married King George III.

(14)   **Charlotte County, Florida.** This county was named by the English in 1775, for the Bay of Charlotte Harbor, in tribute to Queen Charlotte, wife of King George III.

(15)   **Charlotte, Illinois.** An unincorporated community in Livingston County, Illinois, United States

(16)   **Charlottetown, Canada.** This city was established in 1764, on the south shore of Prince Edward Island, Canada. The city was established by Captain Samuel Holland, who suggested the city be one of the primary Island towns in honor of Queen Charlotte, wife of George III of England.

(17)   **Mecklenburg, Virginia.** In 1762, the Virginia Assembly chartered the town of Mecklenburg, in honor of Queen Charlotte from Mecklenburg Strelitz, Germany.

(18)   **Queen Charlotte Track, New Zealand.** English explorer, Captain James Cook, on the HMS Endeavour ship named the "Queen Charlotte Sound" in New Zealand. This was the start of the Queen Charlotte Track, January 17, 1770. [232] The area offers coastal views of New Zealand and has walking and biking with resorts, lodges, food and wine.

Places Named for Queen Charlotte

(19) **Ca Charlotte, Sud, Haiti** is a town near Port-au-Prince, Haiti.

(20) **Charlotte, Artibonite region, Haiti.** Another town near Port au Prince, Haiti.

(21) **Charlotte Village, Sierra Leone.** The town of Charlotte is in a mountainous village in the Rural District, Western Area of Sierra Leone. It is located about twenty miles outside Freetown, Sierra Leone's capital. Charlotte Village is close to the towns of Regent, and Leicester. The main economic activity in Charlotte is farming.

(22) **Fort Charlotte, St. Lucia.** This Fort began under the French and was continued by the British. It was the location of fierce fighting between the French and British in colonial times. Fort buildings have been renovated as the Sir Arthur Lewis Community College.

(23) **Charlotte, Distrito Especial en Colombia, South America.** The community of Charlotte is a part of Bogota, Columbia.

Statues in Charlotte, North Carolina

There are two statues of Queen Charlotte in the City of Charlotte, North Carolina. The first statue is called "Queen Charlotte Walks in Her Garden." It stands in front of the World Trade Center on North College Street, corner of East 5th Street in Charlotte. The Statue was designed by sculptor/physician Bailey Graham Weathers, Jr and is preserved and maintained by Bank of America, in Mecklenburg County, North Carolina.[233] The dog represented in the artwork shows Queen Charlotte's love of pets, and the sculpture showed her hair thick and braided, thus revealing her Moorish/Black heritage.

Places Named for Queen Charlotte

Statue in Charlotte, North Carolina: Queen Charlotte with Her Dogs, by Sculptor Bailey Graham Weathers, Jr.[234]

Inscription for Sculpture in Charlotte, North Carolina
"Queen Charlotte Walks in Her Garden"

"QUEEN CHARLOTTE WALKS IN HER GARDEN / GRAHAM WEATHERS / SCULPTOR AMERICAN 1988 / IN 1761, COLONIAL AMERICANS WERE FASCINATED BY THE ROYAL / WEDDING OF ENGLANDS KING GEORGE III TO A 17-YEAR OLD GERMAN / PRINCESS. CHARLOTTE SOPHIA OF THE DUCHY OF MECKLENBURG-STRELITZ / SETTLERS HERE WERE REBELLIOUS TOWARD THE KING AND HIS AGENTS BUT / NAMED THEIR TOWN AND COUNTY IN HER HONOR, IN HOPES OF GAINING / ROYAL FAVOR. / SHE WAS A SMALL WOMAN "EASY, GENTEEL, AND AGREEABLE," WHO / BORE 15 CHILDREN, PLAYED THE HARPSICHORD, LEARNED BOTANY, AND / TOOK PLEASURE IN KEW AND RICHMOND GARDENS. HER DOGS, ONE NAMED / PRESTO, FOLLOWED HER ON DAILY WALKS. HER APPEARANCE AND / INFORMAL APPAREL ARE MODELED AFTER PORTRAITS IN ENGLISH MUSEUMS. / KING GEORGE III, PLAGUED BY RECURRING ILLNESS, CALLED HER / "MY PHYSICIAN MY FRIEND" SHE IS REMEMBERED AS A GREAT BENEFACTOR / OF HOSPITALS. QUEEN CHARLOTTE WAS THE GRANDMOTHER OF QUEEN VICTORIA. / "SHE IS FULL OF SENSE AND GRACIOUSNESS. MINGLED WITH DELICACY OF / MIND AND LIVELINESS OF TEMPER" / FANNY BURNEY, COURT ATTENDANT AND NOVELIST OF THE PERIOD. / "A MOST AGREEABLE COUNTENANCE, VASTLY GENTEEL, WITH AN AIR / NOT WITHSTANDING HER BEING A LITTLE WOMAN. TRULY MAJESTIC." /

A NOBLEWOMAN REPORTS THE QUEEN'S CORONATION, 1761.

Places Named for Queen Charlotte

A second statue created in 1990 by artist Raymond Kaskey, originally stood in front of the Charlotte-Douglas International Airport, in Charlotte, North Carolina. The statue showed a figure that was supposed to be Queen Charlotte, blowing in a wind gust produced by an airplane, while holding up a crown to represent the "Queen City" of Charlotte, NC. For some reason, the statue was very unpopular as evidenced by its listing on a website as "12 of the World's Ugliest Statues."[235] Due to the controversy surrounding the design, the statue was moved from the front of the Charlotte-Douglass airport, in Charlotte, North

Carolina, to a location that in Y'2016, stood in-between daily parking decks, on a white column surrounded by decorative landscaping. It is not known if the real dislike for the statue was connected to dislike for Queen Charlotte, or for the design.

Statue of Queen Charlotte, by artist Raymond Kaskey

Sign of the Queen," New York Restaurant

In 1762, in New York City, a restaurant called "Sign of the Queen" was established in honor of Queen Charlotte, by a free man named Samuel Fraunces (circa 1722-1792). The popular restaurant owner was known as "Black Sam," and he was from the West Indies. Black Sam was President George Washington's favorite Chef and he worked for the President when the seat of the Colonial government was in Philadelphia, Pennsylvania. Although most historians believe

CHAPTER THIRTEEN
Places Named for Queen Charlotte

Black Sam was of mixed race, like Charlotte he is another example of a person where there is some debate over whether he was black or white.

Black Sam established a restaurant in New York during the time the British occupied New York, during the Revolutionary War. He fed Revolutionary soldiers at the restaurant and General George Washington was a regular guest. When he opened the restaurant, it was called, 'Sign of the Queen' Tavern, but within a year it was better known as the 'Queen's Head Tavern.' Sam posted a portrait of the Queen on the wall so, he knew what Charlotte looked like. Given Black Sam's mixed race based on his appearance in his portrait, it is very interesting that he named his restaurant after Queen Charlotte. Perhaps he saw the Queen's picture when Lord Dunmore passed around the colonies, and recognized her as a woman, with a heritage similar to his own.

Samuel Fraunces, known as Black Sam named his New York Restaurants "Sign of the Queen Restaurant" and Queen's Head Tavern[236]

CHAPTER FOURTEEN
Caregiver and End of An Era

King George III is often referred to as "Mad King George." Movies and books have ridiculed him for centuries because many believe he suffered from a mental illness. It is true that King George III developed his severe and unpredictable illness, some years after the American Revolutionary War. First reports of something wrong were in October 1788, at Kew Gardens when he complained of pains in his stomach and legs and became feverish. Author Olwen Hedley wrote that the staff of the Royal Family reported the King talked endlessly and became out of control. His illness escalated beyond his physical pain and appeared to be a mental disorder.[237]

Later, a diagnosis of the King's health disorder was determined to be a physical, genetic blood disorder called "porphyria" that includes aches, pains, and blue urine.[238] The Mayo Institute defines porphyria as an illness with two major components: (1) affect of the nervous system, and (2) "cutaneous," a disease that mainly affects the skin. Some types of porphyria have both nervous system and skin symptoms, and others have mainly one or the other. Acute porphyria can cause severe nervous system symptoms which appear quickly and can be life-threatening. Symptoms may last one to two weeks and usually improve slowly after the attack.[239]

Other modern researchers believe King George III had bi-polar disorder, given his erratic bursts of loud talking and uncontrollable behavior. However, not all agree with the "Mad King George" designation as indicated in 1972, when His Royal Highness Prince Charles wrote a foreword for a book titled, <u>King George III.</u> Prince Charles wrote, "modern medical knowledge and research have enabled doctors to study the physician's reports on the King's health…and to produce diagnosis to show that the King's mental state during his attacks was in keeping with mental states due to infections, toxic processes, and metabolic disturbances." His Royal Highness continued, "the important point is that the King suffered from attacks of a physical disease. There is no evidence that he was schizophrenic, or depressive, or that he suffered from syphilis of the center nervous system....I think there can now be little doubt that George III suffered from periodic attacks of a metabolic illness."[240]

Yet, other theories suggest the King may have been poisoned by herbal medicine based on gentian--a plant, with deep blue flowers that is used today as a mild tonic and turns urine blue.[241] Note: the plant "Gentiana acaulis" is grown today at the Rock Garden in Kew Gardens. While it is not known if the gentian plant was at Kew during the time of King George III, the leaves of Gentiana acaulis are used in contemporary medicine. In the 21st century, the plant is held at Kew's Economic Botany Collection, where botanists can access them.[242]

King George III, painted by Johan Zoffany, 1771 [243]

Regarding of the actual diagnosis King George was extremely sick. During his illness, King George III rallied periodically and was able to make public appearances with Queen Charlotte, his daughters, and sons. However, since people during his era did not understand mental illness he was treated badly in the press. In January 1789, the King's condition improved and despite certain eccentric characteristics, it appeared that he made a full recovery in March of the same year. Treatments prescribed by his doctors and his apparent courageous triumph over the affliction added greatly to his popularity. However, as he aged, he suffered recurrences.[244] When he appeared normal, he still suffered from serious bouts of mental instability and emotional tirades. In 1801, British medical professionals determined he was permanently deranged and in 1810, it was determined he was mentally unfit to rule during the last decade of his reign.

CHAPTER FOURTEEN
Caregiver and End of An Era

Queen as Caregiver

As his wife and caregiver, Charlotte worked with doctors to provide him with care at Windsor Palace. There are no reports of the Queen betraying her husband, mistreating him or getting involved with someone else. Queen Charlotte was loving and loyal. Sadly, over time King George III became blind, deaf and unable to recognize his own family and held conversations with imaginary people—some of whom were dead. He reported talked a lot with Octavius, the baby son he and Charlotte had lost in infancy from smallpox. When the King experienced his mental crises, his physician Sir George Baker M.D, restricted him to his rooms in isolation and restrained him in strait jackets.[245]

As the King's illness worsened his son George IV, the Prince of Wales petitioned the Parliament to appoint him Regent, which would have made him the acting king. Queen Charlotte was furious with her son's lack of compassion and loyalty and she fought him at every turn. She thought George IV was selfish and extravagant and was not prepared to replace his father as King of England. Lady in Waiting Fanny Burney wrote in her journal that Queen Charlotte had the duel difficulties of handling the King's loud talking, intermittent attacks, and violence, while at the same time dealing with the internal tension caused by the Prince. [246] Over a period of years, many debates took place in the British Parliament about the King's fitness to serve. A "Regency Bill" was put before the Parliament and for months, the Queen didn't know if or when a decision would be made to take power from the King, and to put their son George IV, in charge.[247]

When the King did have periods of normalcy he was able to visibly rule England with Charlotte and his daughters by his side. Despite his son's betrayal, King George III was able to reassure the British people that he was still in charge. Queen Charlotte intervened on his behalf in many matters of government from 1788, when his illness began, until her death in 1818. She protected the King's public image; handled oversight of his medical care; and interfaced with Parliament. She was his legal guardian and kept their large family together. Charlotte became expert at operating behind the scenes and found ways to have her opinions known on many issues, including abolition of slavery.

Biographer Thomas Williams commented, "Indeed early in the reign there were suspicions entertained that her Majesty was not averse to interfere in politics, but while the King preserved his health and intellects, she had the prudence to keep in the background."[248] In other words, when the King was healthy and in charge, Queen Charlotte stayed in the background but, when he

Caregiver and End of An Era

became ill, the power shifted to her—not her son. Sadly, when King George III lost his physical and mental powers and became blind, and mentally ill. Charlotte had to care for him during a prolonged period. But, somehow she held onto the throne, with the help of other children, who opposed their brother George IV. On January 29, 1820, King George III died at Windsor Castle, after a reign of almost 60 years - the second longest in British history. He outlived his wife Queen Charlotte, who died in 1818.

Queen Charlotte In Her Final Days

Portrait by Sir Thomas Lawrence, of Queen Charlotte, during her older years[249]

When Queen Charlotte was 74 years old, she grew frail and started experiencing physical difficulties. Her legs swelled, her joints grew sore and she contracted pneumonia. Although her health was failing she continued her duties in the Court and served as caregiver for her husband. By spring 1818, Queen Charlotte retired from public life and moved to Kew Palace to try to regain her strength. But, as the year wore on, her health deteriorated swiftly. Unfortunately, during this time she and King George III were living at different places, since both of them were ill. This was distressing to Queen Charlotte, since she could not see her beloved husband of five decades.

During her times of struggle, Queen Charlotte was able to survive partially due to her dedication to her faith. Per the 1819 "Brief Memoir" by Thomas Williams, "her Majesty had always set a laudable example by her attendance upon public worship; and during the last month of her illness, we are told, prayers were read daily in her chamber, and she receive the holy sacrament from the hands of the Archbishop himself." [250] On November 17, 1818, Charlotte settled in a

Caregiver and End of An Era

comfortable armchair with all of her children—around her and quietly passed away. Her eldest son George IV, the Prince Regent was there and he was finally able to assume the power of the throne. Reportedly, he held Queen Charlotte's hand as she sat in an armchair at Kew Palace.

Queen Charlotte was buried at St George's Chapel, at Windsor Castle, one of her favorite places. She is recorded as the second longest-serving Queen in British history. She was married to King George III from September 8, 1761 to her death November 17, 1818—a total of 57 years, and 70 days. Her eldest son, the Prince Regent, claimed Charlotte's jewels at her death, but the rest of her property was sold at auction from May to August 1819. Her clothes, furniture, and even her snuff were sold by Christie's Auction House. Selling the Queen's personal items seemed rather harsh but, those were the decisions made by her children. Perhaps getting rid of the Queens property contributed to her overlooked image in history, thus rendering her the "Invisible Queen."

Sadly, King George III, who was still suffering from his illnesses, including dementia, never learned about his beloved wife's death. He died blind, deaf, lame and suffering, 14 months after Charlotte's death.

Epilogue

This book is titled, "Invisible Queen" because it reflects the fact that very little is known in the general public about Queen Sophia Charlotte of Mecklenburg-Streliz. Her reputation is limited even though she had many personal accomplishments and talents. Many people with far fewer achievements than Queen Charlotte, are remembered in folklore and history.

This author believes Queen Charlotte made significant contributions to England, the Royal Family and the world, and that she has been ignored primarily due to her mixed-race ancestry, that is traced to Moorish/Black heritage. Cynics claim Queen Charlotte was pure Caucasian and German, and not mixed with Portuguese/Moorish heritage as asserted by Mario de Valdes y Cocum and historian J.A. Rodgers. However, when the reader views portraits of Charlotte's mother Princess Elizabeth Albertina, her brother Duke Adolph Frederick IV and portraits of Charlotte they should see evidence of a mixed race heritage in their faces.

Even though Queen Charlotte has been overlooked in a lot of British, American and European history the fact she was of mixed race heritage—like millions of American Whites, Latinos, African Americans, Europeans, South Americans, Asians, Africans and many other nationalities, should be viewed as an enriching asset that can bring people together in appreciation of the power of diversity. It is the author's hope that through this book, along with other recent works, history will be corrected and that an accurate story about Queen Sophia Charlotte can inspire young people all over the world, regardless of their backgrounds and racial heritage.

When Charlotte moved from her small rural kingdom, of Mecklenburg Strelitz, Germany to marry King George III, in England, it was within weeks of her mother passing away. Since Charlotte lived under a system that required young girls to accept arranged marriages without any role in the decision-making, Charlotte left home at the age of 17, to marry a man she had never met. When she arrived in England, she became acquainted with her new mother-in-law, husband and members of the Court and instead of having panic attacks, she stepped up to her new and enormous responsibilities as the Queen of England. Her example is excellent for young people who are under pressures…you too can handle it!

In 1994, in America a film titled "The Madness of King George" was produced. The film featured a talented blond actress who played the part of Queen Charlotte. One could not tell from the film's portrayal of Charlotte that she had Moorish/African heritage or a "true mulatto face," as Baron Stockmar, a member of the Royal Court observed. For over 200+ years, the misrepresentation of Queen Charlotte's Moorish/African heritage has deprived citizens of the world—particularly people of African heritage, youth and women—a true picture of King George III, his loving, caring wife of 57 years and their 15 children.

During the 1700's -1800's when Queen Charlotte lived, there were low expectations for women, in Europe, the American colonies and the world. Women were not educated—no matter their rank in society, However, Queen Sophia Charlotte's parents made sure Charlotte was educated, and given lessons in music, and art. It was unusual given the time that Charlotte lived, for women to go to school but, Charlotte's parents put a priority on education for their sons and daughters and prepared them to be leaders. This is a good lesson for parents everywhere—educate your children and make sure they are prepared for the challenges ahead. While they might not become Kings or Queens, youth need to be prepared for leadership. They need to know how to work alongside the scholars of their time, the way Queen Charlotte worked with explorer Joseph Banks, Prime Minister Earl Bute, astronomer Caroline Hershel and artist Mary Mosur.

Most importantly, Queen Charlotte supported the Abolitionist movement in England and took positions on behalf of the Royal Family, that openly opposed slavery. Her support for abolitionists Granville Sharp and William Wilberforce helped their decades long fight, to end the violent, brutal practice of slavery in England. Finally, in 1808, while King George III and Queen Charlotte were still on the throne, the Parliament legally ended slavery in England and Queen Charlotte and her daughters publicly celebrated.

While some may criticize the Queen for serving on the throne during the time slavery was in practice, she did oppose it. It would have been difficult for her to leave the throne or to openly fight against King George III and the Parliament over the abominable practice. As Queen, Charlotte could have spent all of her days in official Court duties that included wearing fabulous gowns, having her hair done and hosting official parties. She could have ignoring the suffering of African people who were in bondage in England, the West Indies, and the Americas. Instead, she supported Abolitionist leaders who opposed slavery until it was abolished in England. Yes, it took most of Queen Charlotte's life for England's to outlaw slavery but, end it was outlawed. In the future, the world should hope other wives of world leaders have the integrity and resolve that Queen Charlotte had—even if takes decades to change society and to create a better, freer, safer world for all.

Appendix

Prince Charles becomes patron of Royal Botanic Gardens
Zap Gossip News, 26 July 2016

Prince Charles, of England

Princes Charles has become a patron of the Royal Botanic Gardens at Kew.

The 67-year-old Royal is "delighted" to be an official supporter of the gardens in southwest London and is "proud" of its history spanning over 25 decades.

He said: "I have always had the greatest affection and admiration for the Royal Botanic Gardens at Kew, so I could not be more proud and delighted to have been invited to become Patron of this great institution. Kew has had its roots planted deeply in British soil for more than 250 years, but has developed an international reputation as one of the world's greatest botanic gardens, renowned for its scientific research and plant collections."

And Kew director, Richard Deverell commented: "It is a truly great honor to welcome The Prince as our Patron and we look forward to sharing our many exciting plans for a future in which Kew plays a very central role in the conservation and sustainability of our precious planet."

Charles - who has long been passionate about the impact of climate change and global warming - hopes that the new Great Broad Walk Borders will help to stress the importance to protect the "unique plants" of the world from extinction.

He added: "The new Great Broad Walk Borders are a great way to celebrate the diversity of the plant kingdom in all its astonishing richness - particularly at a time when, as scientists at Kew have recently stressed, so many of the world's unique plants are under constant threat of extinction. I very much hope that the new borders will attract even more visitors and encourage them to learn about Kew's exciting role at the heart of global efforts to unlock why plants matter."

Note to Readers: Described below is the copyright law in the UK that provides authorization for the use of photos used in this book
Copyright Law Fact Sheet in the UK

Issued: 5th July 2004; Last amended: 5 July 2004
National copyright laws stipulate the duration of copyright, and the actual duration will vary between nation states. The content of this fact sheet reflects the provisions of the Berne Convention and should be regarded as a rough guide only.

1. Typical duration of legal copyright protection: Normal protection provided by the Berne Convention is life of the author plus fifty years from death, with the following exceptions:
   - Film, cinematographic work:
     50 years from the making of the work, or if made available to the public within the 50 years, (i.e. by publication or performance), 50 years from the date the author first makes the work available to the public.
   - Anonymous works: 50 years from the date made available to the public.
   - Artistic works, such as photographs and applied art:
     At least 25 years from creation.

   In all cases, individual national laws can, and often will, allow additional protection over and above the terms of the Convention. For example, in the UK most work is protected for the life of the author plus 70 years. The Convention sets out what authors can realistically expect. There are also exceptions allowed for countries bound by the Rome Act.
   Once a work is in the public domain it is available to all. You cannot stop others using the work and you will have no claim to copyright on the work.

This fact sheet is intended only as an introduction to ideas and concepts only. It should not be treated as a definitive guide, nor should it be considered to cover every area of concern, or be regarded as legal advice.

Retrieved: https://www.copyrightservice.co.uk/copyright/p10_duration

References and Sources

Andrews, Tina, "Charlotte Sophia Myth, Madness and the Moor," (2001)

Atlanta Black Star website: http://atlantablackstar.com/2015/10/14/meet-sophia-charlotte-first-black-queen-england/

Burney, Frances, "Diary of Frances Burney," (1840)

Brendlinger, Irv. A., "Anthony Benezet, The True Champion of the Slave," (1996), http://digitalcommons.georgefox.edu/truths_bright

Brook, John, "King George III," (1972)

Cocom, Mario de Valdes, "Blurred Racial Lines of Famous Families," Public Broadcasting System, http://www.pbs.org/wgbh/pages/frontline/ shows/secret/famous/ Royalfamily.html

Groom, Susanne and Prosser, Lee, "Kew Palace, the Official Illustrated History" (2006)

Hedley, Olwen, Queen Charlotte, (1975)

Hudson, Kimba, Mulatto Queen, (2014)

K'Orinda-Yimbo, Akinyi Von, Darkest Europe and Africa's Nightmare: A Critical Observation of the Neighbouring Continents, Algora Publishing, 2008

Madge. Tim, Royal Yachts of the World, (2003)

Papendiek, Charlotte Louise, Court and Private Life in the Time of Queen Charlotte: Being the..., Volume 2, Publisher, Richard Bentley and Sons, 1797-98.

Pearse, Joysetta Marsh and Fatimah White, "Black Royals, Queen Charlotte," (2014)

Powell, Angelika S. and Jean L. Cooper, Queen Charlotte, 1744-1818: A Bilingual Exhibit, University of Virginia, On-Line, http://people.virginia.edu/~jlc5f/charlotte/english_intro.html

Rodgers, J.A, Nature Knows No Color Line, (1952)

Ryan, Thomas, History of Queen's Lying In Hospital, (1885)

Scobie, Edward, Black Britannia: A History of Blacks in Britain, (1972)

Tillyard, Stella, A Royal Affair: George III and his Troublesome Siblings, (2007)

Winfield, Rif. British Warships of the Age of Sail *1714–1792; (*2008)

Watkins, John, Memoirs of Her Most Excellent Majesty, Sophia Charlotte, 1792-1831; (2013)

Zap Gossip News, London, 26 July 2016, "Prince Charles becomes patron of Royal Botanic Gardens"

Web Sites About Queen Charlotte

People of Color in European Art History:
http://medievalpoc.tumblr.com/post/70933483399/cerberusia-medievalpoc-queen-charlotte

African American Registry
http://www.aaregistry.org/historic_events/view/englands-first-black-queen-sophie-charlotte-born

The Guardian
https://www.theguardian.com/world/2009/mar/12/race-monarchy

Laura Purcell: The Not Black Queen
http://laurapurcell.com/the-not-black-queen/

The House of Hanover
http://www.englishmonarchs.co.uk/hanover_14.html

The Mulatto Diaries
https://mulattodiaries.com/2010/07/08/conspicuously-negroid-features/

The Hook
http://www.readthehook.com/98341/cover-was-queen-charlotte-black

Englands Black Queens
https://erinlawless.wordpress.com/2013/01/02/englands-black-queens/

Footnotes

Instructions for readers: Each footnote takes you to a source that provide more information about the subject in the book. In many cases, there is a web address that you can put into an Internet search engine, to learn more about the subject at hand.

[1] http://www.historytoday.com/michael-bloch/Royal-weddings-englands-ruritania
[2] Williams, Thomas, A Brief Memoir of Her Late Majesty Queen Charlotte, pg 2
[3] Oulton, W.C. Authentic and Impartial Memoirs of her Late Majesty Charlotte, Queen of Great Britain and Ireland, pg 9
[4] www.Royaltyguide.nl/families/mecklenbutg/mecklenburgstrelitz1.htm
[5] Hedley, Olwen, Queen Charlotte, pg. 28.
[6] Convent in Wesphalia, http://www.hanse.org/en/hanseatic-cities/herford.php
[7] Definition of canoness. http://www.merriam-webster.com/dictionary/canoness
[8] Hedly, Olwen, Queen Charlotte, pg 29.
[9] The Burney Center at McGill University. Retrieved from http://burneycentre.mcgill.ca/bio_frances.html
[10] Shared Photo, courtesy of Ingo Kirschnereit, commons.wikimedia.org/wiki/User:Cyclejakob

[11] Hedley, Olwen, pg 29)
[12] http://www.biography.com/people/voltaire-9520178#major-works
[13] http://www.britannica.com/EBchecked/topic/255802/harpsichord
[14] http://www.newworldencyclopedia.org/entry/Frederick_II_of_Prussia
[15] http://www.history.com/topics/seven-years-war
[16] Williams, Thomas, A Brief Memoir of Her Late Majesty Queen Charlotte, 1819, pgs 4 & 5
[17] On-Line Etymology Dictionary. www.etymonline.com/index.php?allowed_in_frame=0&search=Mir&searchmode=none
[18] https://en.wikipedia.org/wiki/Mirow#/media/File:Mirow_Schloss.jpg
[19] http://www.mecklenburg-strelitz.org/georg-alexander-herzog-zu-mecklenburg.html#.VU_nIJPnog4
[20] http://www.mecklenburg-strelitz.org/residences-mirow.html#.V2cWLRZle3Q
[21] http://www.germanplaces.com/germany/mecklenburg-lake-district.html
[22] http://schwarzstorchberingung.de/page11.php
[23] http://www.wanderfreunde-eddelak.de/SCHWERIN/Schwerin_Vogelperspektive.jpg
[24] http://www.mecklenburg-strelitz.org/history-overview.html#.Ve79dJfnotE
[25] Photo retrieved from Creative Commons Attribution-ShareAlike License, Wilipedia, 2016.
[26] http://www.newadvent.org/cathen/10107a.htm
[27] Hedley, Olwen, Queen Charlotte, pg 28
[28] http://www.africaspeaks.com/reasoning/index.php?topic=1513.0;wap2
[29] http://www.englishmonarchs.co.uk/hanover_14.html
[30] https://en.oxforddictionaries.com/definition/moor
[31] http://www.britannica.com/topic/Moor-people
[32] http://www.localhistories.org/portugal.html
[33] Daniel Woge, ca. 1750; Royal Collection Trust 402454
[34] http://www.pbs.org/wgbh/pages/frontline/shows/secret/famous/Royalfamily.html
[35] Cocum, Mario de Valdes y, PBS Front Line, Blurred racial lines of Famous Famililes, http://www.pbs.org/wgbh/pages/frontline/shows/secret/famous/royalfamily.html
[36] PBS Front Line. http://www.pbs.org/wgbh/pages/frontline/shows/secret/famous/Royalfamily.html
[37] Rodgers, J.A., Nature Knows No Color Line, 1952, published by Helga M. Rodgers
[38] Rodgers, J.A., Sex and Race, Volume I, 1940
[39] Walpole, Horace, Letter to Horace Mann, September 10, 1761
[40] Stockmar, Ernst Alfred Christian, Memoirs of Baron Stockmar, University of California Libraries, 1872
[41] https://www.merriam-webster.com/dictionary/mulatto
[42] Weathers, Dr. B. Graham; http://www.brevardstation.com/weathers2.html
[43] Retrieved from Harvard Gazette, http://news.harvard.edu/gazette/story/2010/12/one-drop-rule-persists/
[44] http://www.bbc.co.uk/arts/yourpaintings/artists/allan-ramsay
[45] http://www.Royalcollection.org.uk/collection/400893/frederick-prince-of-wales-1707-1751 by Jean-Étienne Liotard (1702-1789)
[46] Brooke, John, King George III, 1972, pg 15
[47] http://www.historytoday.com/richard-cavendish/death-frederick-prince-wales
[48] Retrieved from the Internet, http://www.englishmonarchs.co.uk/hanover_18.html
[49] http://www.englishmonarchs.co.uk/prince_wales.html
[50] Tillyard, Stella, A Royal Affair: George III and his Troublesome Siblings
[51] Tillyard, Stella, A Royal Affair: George III and his Troublesome Siblings
[52] Pendered, Mary L., The Fair Quaker, Hannah Lightfoot, 1911

[53] Pendered, Mary L., The Fair Quaker, Hannah Lightfoot, 1911
[54] http://www.regencyhistory.net/2014/03/the-Royal-academy-of-arts.html
[55] Hedley, Owen, pg. 4-6
[56] Williams, Thomas, A Brief Memoir of Her Late Majesty Queen Charlotte with Authentic Anecdotes, 1819, pg 3
[57] National Portrait Gallery, London
[58] Grand Ducal House of Mecklenburg Strelitz. https://www.flickr.com/photos/mecklenburg-strelitz/albums/72157630803446370; Artist unknown
[59] Hedley, Owen,
[60] http://www.quakersintheworld.org/quakers-in-action/250
[61] Hedley, Owen, Queen Charlotte, Page 13.
[62] Brooke, John, King George III, pg. 82
[63] Cleverly, Elder John (1712-1777), artist of picture of HMY Royal Yacht Charlotte
[64] Hedley, Owen, Queen Charlotte, pg 19
[65] Hedley, Owen, Queen Charlotte,
[66] http://quatr.us/medieval/architecture/westminsterabbey.htm
[67] Hedley, Owen, Queen Charlotte, pg 51
[68] http://www.britannica.com/biography/Allan-Ramsay-Scottish-painter
[69] www.historytoday.com/richard-cavendish/coronation-george-iii#sthash.p65zkcHz.dpuf
[70] Wilkinson, R., Coronation Banquet of George III and Queen Charlotte, http://www.Royalcollection.org.uk/collection/750457/coronation-banquet-of-george-iii-and-queen-charlotte-in-westminster-hall-1761
[71] http://artgallery.yale.edu/collections/objects/91605
[72] Hedley, Owen, Appendix 3. Crown based on frame in London Museum, located 1956.
[73] http://www.roman-empire.net/articles/article-016.html
[74] http://www.newworldencyclopedia.org/entry/Aleutian_Islands
[75] Hedley, Owen, Queen Charlotte, pg. 56.
[76] http://www.religioustolerance.org/quaker1.htm
[77] Thoms, William, Queen Charlotte and Chevalier D'EON, 1867, pg 15
[78] http://www.mayoclinic.org/diseases-conditions/porphyria/basics/symptoms/con-20028849
[79] http://www.imdb.com/title/tt0110428/
[80] http://www.sciencemuseum.org.uk/broughttolife/people/georgethethird
[81] www.Royal.gov.uk/TheRoyalResidences/BuckinghamPalace/History.aspx
[82] http://www.hrp.org.uk/KewPalace/sightsandstories/buildinghistory/queencharlotte
[83] Quagga Photo by http://www.inetours.com/England/London/pages/Kew_Royal.html
[84] http://whc.unesco.org/en/list/1084
[85] William Marlow (English, 1740–1813), watercolor http://www.metmuseum.org/toah/works-of-art/25.19.43
[86] http://www.kew.org/visit-kew-gardens/explore/attractions/queen-charlottes-cottage
[87] http://www.petermaas.nl/extinct/speciesinfo/quagga.htm. Image in the public domain.
[88] http://www.travelaboutbritain.com/berkshire/berkshire.php
[89] http://www.windsor.gov.uk/things-to-do/windsor-castle-p43983
[90] https://www.Royalcollection.org.uk/visit/windsorcastle/what-to-see-and-do/queen-marys-dolls-house
[91] This file is licensed under the Creative Commons Attribution-Share Alike 3.0 Unported license. Attribution: Contains Ordnance Survey data © Crown copyright
[92] https://www.Royalcollection.org.uk/visit/frogmorehouse/about

[93] Royal Academy of Arts, London

[94] http://www.racollection.org.uk/ixbin/indexplus?record=ART13018
[95] http://africanhistory.about.com/od/slavery/tp/TransAtlantic001.htm
[96] Abolition Project. Retrieved http://abolition.e2bn.org/people_22.html

[97] Schama, Simon, Rough Crossings: Britain, the Slaves and the American Revolution
[98] http://www.nationalarchives.gov.uk/pathways/blackhistory/rights/slave_free.htm
[99] http://spartacus-educational.com/REsharp.htm
[100] http://www.understandingslavery.com/index.php?option=com_content&view=article&id= 432:charicature-by-james-gillray&catid=144&Itemid=254
[101] http://www.understandingslavery.com/index.php?option=com_content&view=article&id= 432:charicature-by-james-gillray&catid=144&Itemid=254
[102] http://www.britannica.com/EBchecked/topic/119725/Clapham-Sect
[103] http://www.blackpast.org/aah/wilberforce-university-1856
[104] Oulton, W.C., Authentic and Impartial Memoirs of Her Late Majesty, Charlotte, Queen of Great Britain and Ireland, 1819
[105] http://touringohio.com/history/camp-charlotte.html
[106] Schama, Simon, Rough Crossings, pgs 70-75

107 Schama, Simon, Rough Crossings, pg 69
108 http://www.encyclopediavirginia.org/Lord_Dunmore_s_Proclamation_1775
109 http://www.pbs.org/wgbh/pages/frontline/shows/secret/famous/Royalfamily.html
110 http://www.blackpast.org/aah/lord-dunmore-s-proclamation-1775. Proclamation in Public Domain.
111http://docsouth.unc.edu/neh/equiano1/summary.html
112 Dictionary of African Christian Biography: http://www.dacb.org/stories/nigeria/equiano_olaudah.html
113 http://www.quakersintheworld.org/quakers-in-action/60
114 Brendlinger, Irv. A., Anthony Benezet, the True Champion of the Slave
115Alan Ramsey Portrait of Queen Charlotte, http://www.thefamousartists.com/allan-ramsay/queen-charlotte
116 http://www.bbc.co.uk/arts/yourpaintings/artists/allan-ramsay
117 Self portrait by Alan Ramsey, 1761http://www.npg.org.uk/collections/search/person.php?LinkID=mp03703&role=art
118 http://www.nytimes.com/movies/movie/471471/Belle/credits
119 Cocom, Mario de Valdes;   http://www.pbs.org/wgbh/pages/frontline/shows/secret/famous/Royalfamily.html
120http://www.blackloyalist.info/person/display/1485
121 http://www.the-athenaeum.org/art/list.php?m=a&s=tu&aid=2958; public domain
122 http://www.ncbi.nlm.nih.gov/pmc/articles/PMC1200696/
123 http://www.unofficialroyalty.com/royal-illnesses-and-deaths/smallpox-knew-no-class-boundaries/
124 http://www.archontology.org/nations/uk/king_uk/george4a.php
125 http://www.regencyhistory.net/2011/10/frederick-duke-of-york-1763-1827.html
126 William IV from The History of the Life and Reign of William IV , by Robert Huish (1837)
127 Allen, W. Gore (1960). King William IV. London: Cresset Press.
128 http://www.britRoyals.com/kings.asp?id=william4
129 http://www.Royalcollection.org.uk/exhibitions/charlotte-princess-Royal-1766-1828
130 http://www.regencyhistory.net/2012/10/prince-edward-duke-of-kent-1767-1820.html
131 Princess Royal from The Lady's Magazine (1792)
132 http://www.regencyhistory.net/2012/04/six-princesses-princess-augusta-sophia.html
133 http://www.regencyhistory.net/2012/05/princess-elizabeth-artist.html
134 http://www.regencyhistory.net/2013/03/prince-ernest-duke-of-cumberland-and.html
135 http://www.regencyhistory.net/2013/04/augustus-duke-of-sussex-1773-1843.html
136 http://www.regencyhistory.net/2013/04/adolphus-frederick-duke-of-cambridge.html
137 http://www.regencyhistory.net/2013/04/princess-mary.html
138 http://www.regencyhistory.net/2012/06/two-little-princes-prince-octavius-1779.html
139 http://www.regencyhistory.net/2012/05/six-princesses-princess-amelia-1783.html
140 http://www.biography.com/people/james-cook-21210409
141 https://www.nasa.gov/centers/kennedy/shuttleoperations/orbiters/orbitersend.html
142 http://www.history.com/topics/british-history/george-iii
143De Quincy, Thomas Quote: www.Royalcollection.org.uk/george-iii-and-queen-charlotte-patronage-collecting-and-court-taste
144 https://www.Royalcollection.org.uk/collection/922120/frogmore-house-the-queens-library
145 http://www.nationalgallery.org.uk/artists/sir-joshua-reynolds
146 Benjamin West Portrait, hanging at Buckingham Palace, East.
https://www.Royalcollection.org.uk/collection/405405/queen-charlotte-1744-1818
147 http://patrickbaty.co.uk/2011/07/13/kings-observatory-kew/
148 Proceedings of the Royal Society of London, 1885, London, Harrison and Sons, Martins Lane

149 Museum of the History of Science, Broad Street, Oxford
www.mhs.ox.ac.uk/collections/search/displayrecord/?mode=displaymixed&module=ecatalogue&invnumber=35086&irn=6114&query=George%20III
150 Science Museum, Blythe House. Object No. 1965-460. © Science Museum - See more at:
http://www.sciencemuseum.org.uk/online_science/explore_our_collections/objects/index/smxg-8483#na
151 http://www.biography.com/people/caroline-lucretia-herschel-9336995
152 William Hershel photo retrieved from http://www.physics.unlv.edu/~jeffery/astro/astronomer/astronomer.html
153 http://womenshistory.about.com/od/scienceastronomy/p/herschel.htm
154 http://womenshistory.about.com/od/scienceastronomy/p/herschel.htm
155 space-facts.com/uranus/
156 Burney, Frances, The Project Gutenberg EBook of The Diary and Letters of Madame D'Arblay, Vol. 1 (of 3), page 420.
157 http://womenshistory.about.com/od/scienceastronomy/p/herschel.htm
158 Royal Society Publishing, http://rsta.royalsocietypublishing.org/content/373/2039/20140210
159 Farmer George reference: http://www.britishempire.co.uk/biography/georgeiii.htm
160 http://people.virginia.edu/~jlc5f/charlotte/charlotte.html
161 Royal Collection Trust, https://www.Royalcollection.org.uk/collection/421016/queen-charlotte-1744-1818
162 Hedley, Olwen, Queen Charlotte, page179-180
163 https://www.Royalcollection.org.uk/visit/frogmorehouse/about
164 Kew Herbarium, http://www.kew.org/science-conservation/collections/herbarium
165 Newton, Sir Isaac, President of Royal Society, http://www-history.mcs.st-and.ac.uk/Biographies/Newton.html
166 http://plantzafrica.com/plantqrs/strelitziareginae.htm

167 http://catalogue.nla.gov.au/Record/2661854
168 Retrieved from Georgian Index http://www.georgianindex.net/princewaleswedding/Prince_Wales_wedding.html
169 Hedley, Olwen, Queen Charlotte, page 181
170 http://www.tickhillhistorysociety.org.uk/local_snippets_rev_Anderson.asp
171 Archive copy of Flora Scotica. https://archive.org/details/florascoticaorsy02ligh
172 Chambers, Neil, The Letters of Sir Joseph Banks: 1768-1820. Letter 30, 1788.
173 Notes added by Neil Chambers, editing letters by Sir Joseph Banks
174 http://www.britannica.com/biography/John-Stuart-3rd-Earl-of-Bute

175 Royal Collection Trust/© Her Majesty Queen Elizabeth II 2014
http://cdn.Royalcollection.org.uk/cdn/farfuture/J9sZK_QeWZE81mOdvhaF0og_6gYkcuAqHpurHQywcOw/mtime:142338674
9/sites/Royalcollection.org.uk/files/collection-online/b/f/323987-1347638613.jpg.

176 http://www.museumwales.ac.uk/articles/2013-09-30/John-Stuart-3rd-Earl-of-Bute-1713-1792-Butes-Botanical-Tables-/
177 https://www.Royalcollection.org.uk/george-iii-and-queen-charlotte-patronage-collecting-and-court-taste
178 Earl Bute dedication, https://www.Royalcollection.org.uk/collection/1123772/botanical-tables-containing-the-different-familys-of-british-plants
179 https://museum.wales/articles/2013-09-30/John-Stuart-3rd-Earl-of-Bute-1713-1792-Butes-Botanical-Tables-/
180Gearey Caroline, Royal Friendships; The Story of Two Royal Friendships as derived from histories, diaries, biographies, letters etc. London, 1898. pp. 268, 275-276, 284-286.
181 Mary Delany's Pancratium Maritimun from 1775, one of the many botanical collages she made of cut and colored papers on a black ink background.
182 Gearey, Caroline, Royal Friendships; The Story of Two Royal Friendships as derived from histories, diaries, biographies, letters etc. London, 1898. pp. 268, 275-276, 284-286.
183 Gearey Caroline, Royal Friendships; The Story of Two Royal Friendships as derived from histories, diaries, biographies, letters etc. London, 1898. pp. 268, 275-276, 284-286.
184 http://www.kew.org/about/press-media/press-releases/prince-wales-announced-new-Royal-patron-Royal-botanic-gardens-kew
185 http://www.kew.org/about-kew/press-media/press-releases/the-prince-of-wales-announced-as-new-royal-patron-of-royal-0
186 http://www.kew.org/about/press-media/press-releases/prince-wales-announced-new-Royal-patron-Royal-botanic-gardens-kew
187 Holton, Woody, Abigail Adams, pgs 218-129
188 Holton, Woody, Abigail Adams, Pgs 228
189 https://www.monticello.org/site/plantation-and-slavery/appendix-h-sally-hemings-and-her-children
190 National Archives, Retrieved http://founders.archives.gov/documents/Jefferson/99-01-02-3708
191 https://founders.archives.gov/documents/Jefferson/99-01-02-3708
192 http://founders.archives.gov/documents/Franklin/01-19-02-0096
193 http://www.internetstones.com/arcot-diamonds-famous-jewelry.html
194 http://britishlibrary.typepad.co.uk/untoldlives/2012/06/queen-charlottes-arcot-diamonds.html
195 http://britishlibrary.typepad.co.uk/untoldlives/2012/06/queen-charlottes-arcot-diamonds.html
196 http://www.internetstones.com/arcot-diamonds-famous-jewelry.html
197 Scott, Richard Archivist, East India Company Records, http://britishlibrary.typepad.co.uk/untoldlives/2012/06/queen-charlottes-arcot-diamonds.html)

198 Williams, Thomas, A Brief Memoir of Her Majesty Queen Charlotte, 1819
199 http://people.virginia.edu/~jlc5f/charlotte/charlett7.html
200 http://ezitis.myzen.co.uk/queencharlottemarylebone.html
201 Ryan, Thomas; Queen Charlotte's Lying-in Hospital (London, England)
202 Archive Book On-Line: Queen Charlotte's Lying-In-Hospital. https://archive.org/details/historyofqueench00ryan
203 http://pomeranian.org/pomeranian-breed-profile/

204www.germany.travel/en/travel-information/federal-states/bundeslaender_1/mecklenburg-western-pomerania/mecklenburg-vorpommern.html

205 Sir Thomas Gainsborough website, http://www.thomas-gainsborough.org/
206 http://www.electricscotland.com/history/industrial/industry11.htm
207 http://www.electricscotland.com/history/industrial/industry11.htm
208 www.hrp.org.uk/HamptonCourtPalace/stories/palacehighlights/SecretsoftheRoyalbedchamber/TheRoyalbeds#sthash.DbyiMqqL.dpuf
209 https://regencyredingote.wordpress.com/2012/06/01/mrs-phoebe-wrights-celebrated-establishment/
210 https://regencyredingote.wordpress.com/2012/06/01/mrs-phoebe-wrights-celebrated-establishment/
211 https://regencyredingote.wordpress.com/2012/06/01/mrs-phoebe-wrights-celebrated-establishment/

[212] Queen Charlotte's catalog of Books Digitized by New York Public Library, https://archive.org/details/acatalogueguenui00chargoog

[213] http://www.britannica.com/biography/Johann-Christian-Bach

[214] Hedley, Olwen, Queen Charlotte, pg 234, 235

[215] Hedley, Olwen, Queen Charlotte, pg 131

[216] http://people.virginia.edu/~jlc5f/charlotte/mozart.html

[217] http://www.ipl.org/div/mushist/clas/mozart.html

[218] Hedley, Olwen, Queen Charlotte, pg 88-89.

[219] http://www.Royalmint.com/our-coins/ranges/guinea

[220] www.britishmuseum.org/research/collection_online/collection_object_details.aspx?objectId=747991&partId=1&searchText=george+bridgetower&images=true&page=1

[221] Scobie, Edward, Black Britannia, page 110.

[222] Oxford Companion to Food, Alan Davidson [Oxford University Press:Oxford] 1999 (p. 157)

[223] Recipes blend of several on the Internet with substitute ingredients.

[224] http://www.historytoday.com/alison-barnes/first-christmas-tree

[225] http://www.historytoday.com/alison-barnes/first-christmas-tree

[226] First Christmas Tree website, http://www.historytoday.com/alison-barnes/first-christmas-tree

[227] http://Royalcentral.co.uk/blogs/the-Royal-w-holiday-edition-windsor-castle-and-the-christmas-tree-41116

[228] http://www.washingtonpost.com/lifestyle/magazine/the-remarkable-journey-of-a-single-christmas-tree/2011/12/01/gIQALVuZ9O_story.html

[229] http://www.historytoday.com/alison-barnes/first-christmas-tree#sthash.6yTROSIz.dpuf

[230] http://www.people.virginia.edu/~jlc5f/charlotte/charlett1.html

[231] Retrieved from Historical Marker Database http://www.hmdb.org/marker.asp?marker=13499

[232] http://www.qctlc.com/history.html

[233] http://www.meckdec.org/charlotte-liberty-walk

[234] http://docsouth.unc.edu/commland/monument/342/

[235] http://imma1001places.blogspot.com/2011/03/12-of-worlds-ugliest-statues.html

[236] Samuel Fraunces Museum http://frauncestavernmuseum.org/history-and-education/

[237] Hedley, Olwen, Queen Charlotte, pg 141

[238] BBC News, What Was the Truth About the Madness of King George? http://www.bbc.com/news/magazine-22122407

[239] http://www.mayoclinic.org/diseases-conditions/porphyria/basics/symptoms/con-20028849

[240] Brooke, John, King George III, 1974. Foreword by H.R.H. Prince Charles, Prince of Wales

[241] http://www.bbc.com/news/magazine-22122407

[242] http://www.kew.org/science-conservation/plants-fungi/gentiana-acaulis-stemless-gentian

[243] https://www.Royalcollection.org.uk/collection/405072/george-iii-1738-1820

[244] Retrieved from web, "Mad Monarchs", http://madmonarchs.guusbeltman.nl/madmonarchs/george3/george3_bio.htm

[245] Hedley, Olwen, pg 142-145

[246] Hedley, Olwen, pgs 148-150

[247] Hedley, Olwen, pg 168-170

[248] Williams, Thomas, A Brief Memoir of Her Late Majesty Queen Charlotte with Authentic Anecdotes, 1819, pg 28

[249] On display at National Gallery, Trafalgar Square, London London

[250] Williams, Thomas, A Brief Memoir of Her Late Majesty Queen Charlotte, 1819

Index

About the Author

Stephanie E. Myers, Ph.D. is a capacity-building consultant, public relations executive, author, script writer, film producer and civic advocate. With her husband Roy J. Myers, she is Co-Owner and Vice President of R.J. Myers Publishing & Consulting Company, a small, family-owned business, headquartered in the District of Columbia. For 12 years, Dr. Myers served as a Presidential Appointee at federal agencies including the U.S. Department of Commerce, U.S. Department of Health and Human Services and Office of Commercial Space Transportation, U.S. Department of Transportation.

Dr. Myers is a native Californian who lives in Washington, D.C. She is a member of The Links Incorporated, Capital City Chapter; a member of Delta Sigma Theta Public Service Sorority; and is National Co-Chair/Co-Founder of Black Women for Positive Change, originators of the Annual Global Week of Non-Violence, Justice and Opportunities.

She is co-author of the "I Am A Can Do Kid" motivational program for children; Remembering the Path to T-Town: Migration of an African American Family through Seven States to Lincoln, Nebraska 1720-1940; The Rescue of Robby Robo, a children's book; and Invisible Queen, Queen Sophia Charlotte, Queen of England and Ireland, 1761-1818.

Dr. Myers is the proud step-mother of three adult children and Nana to eight grandchildren.